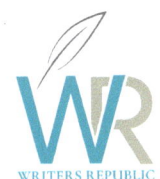

WRITERS REPUBLIC

DONALD G. ENNIS

The Essence of

*Life* and *Beauty*

**WRITERS REPUBLIC L.L.C.**
515 Summit Ave. Unit R1
Union City, NJ 07087, USA

**Website:** *www.writersrepublic.com*
**Hotline:** *1-877-656-6838*
**Email:** *info@writersrepublic.com*

Ordering Information:
Quantity sales. Special discounts are available on quantity purchases by corporations, associations, and others. For details, contact the publisher at the address above.

Library of Congress Control Number:      2023900253
ISBN-13:            979-8-88810-471-2    [Paperback Edition]
                    979-8-88810-843-7    [Hardback Edition]
                    979-8-88810-472-9    [Digital Edition]

Rev. date: 12/15/2022

# The Essence of
# Life and Beauty

DONALD G. ENNIS

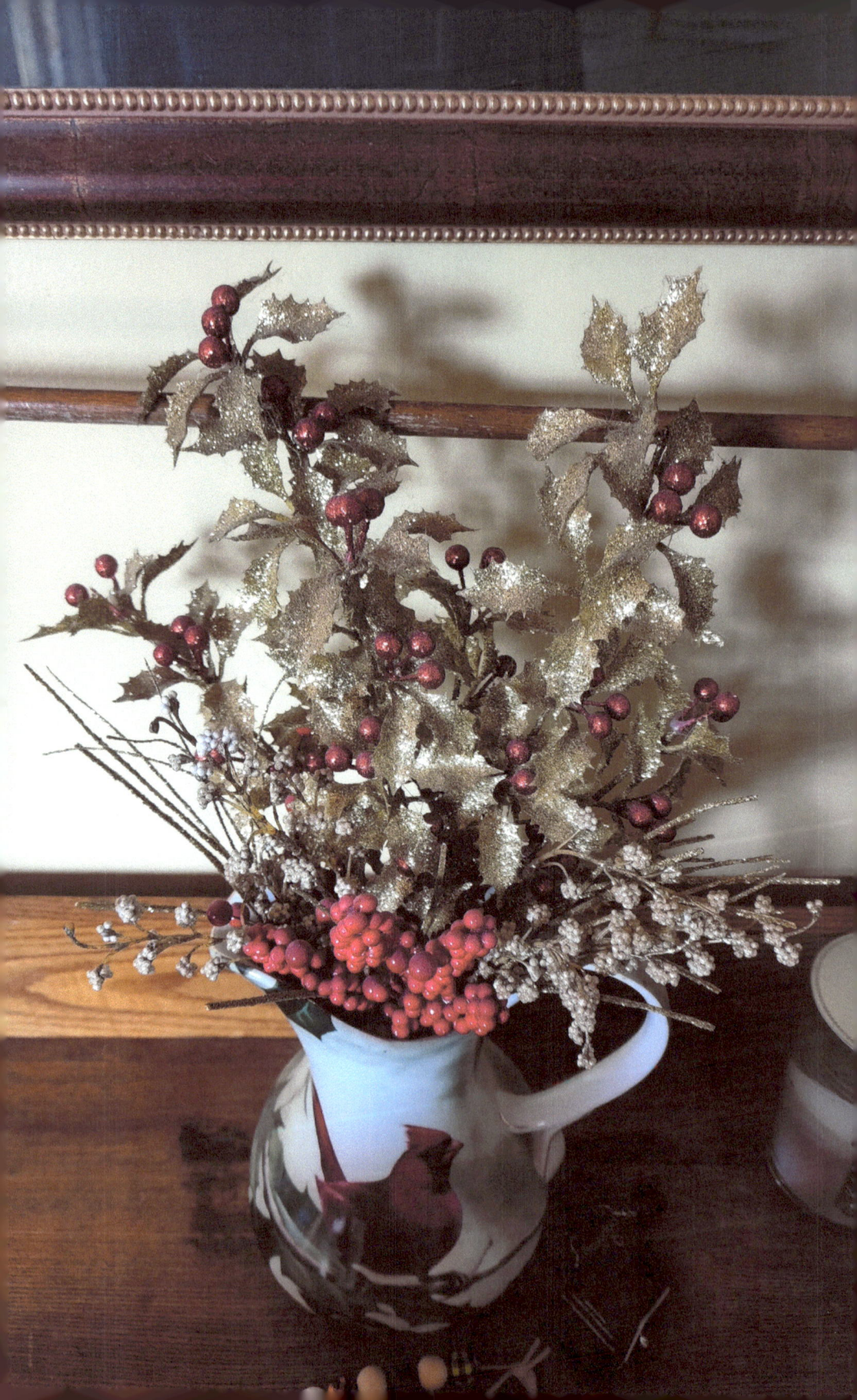

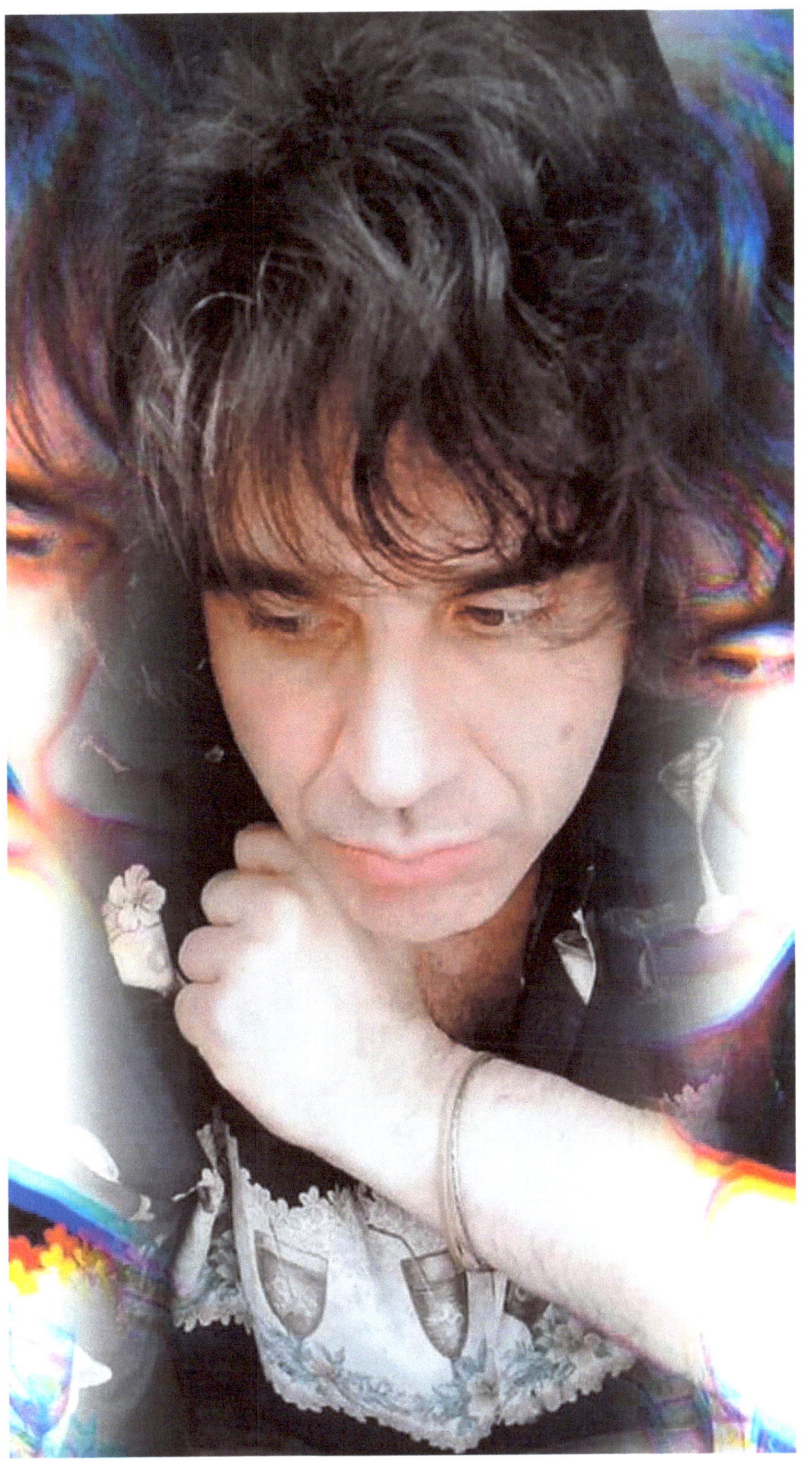

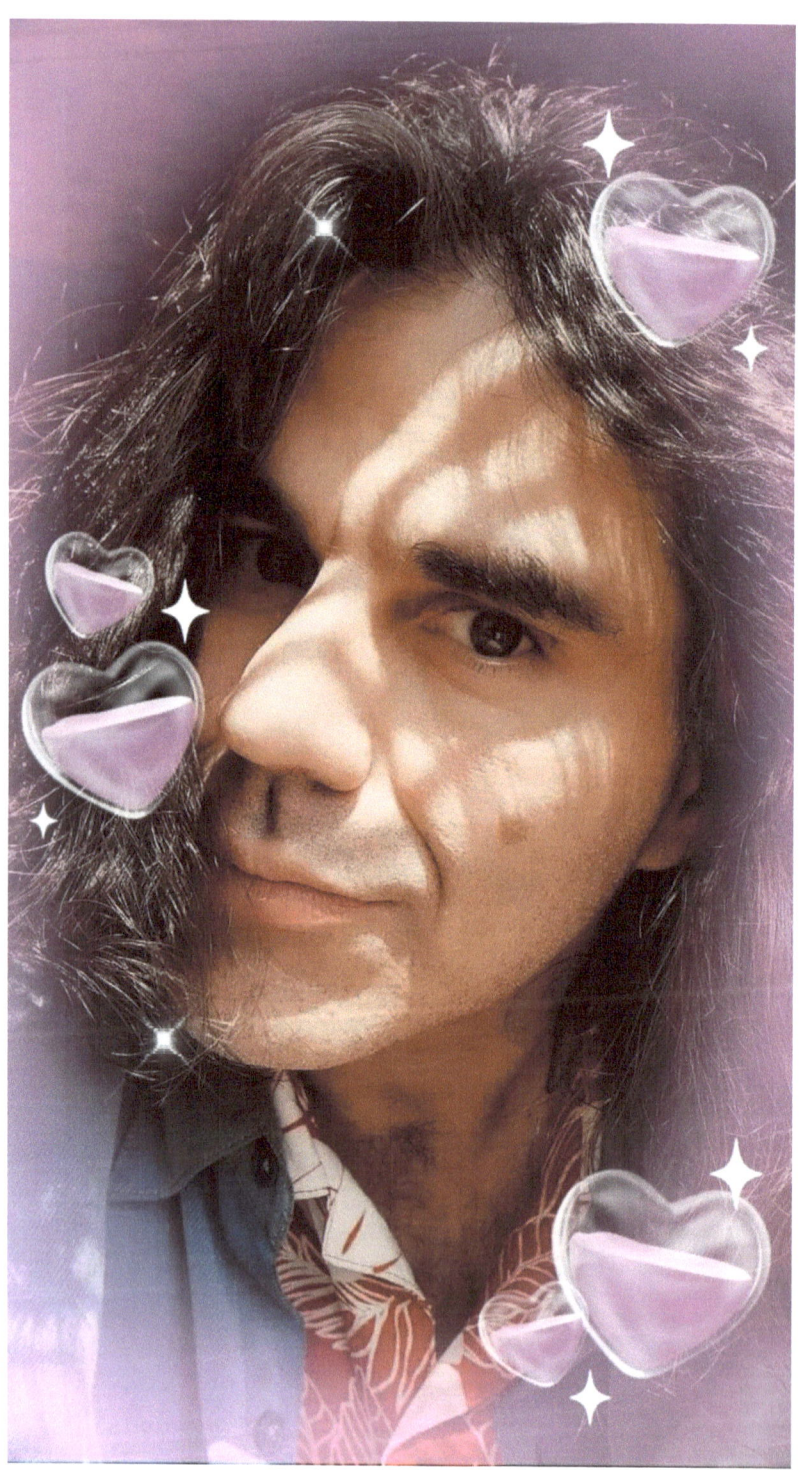

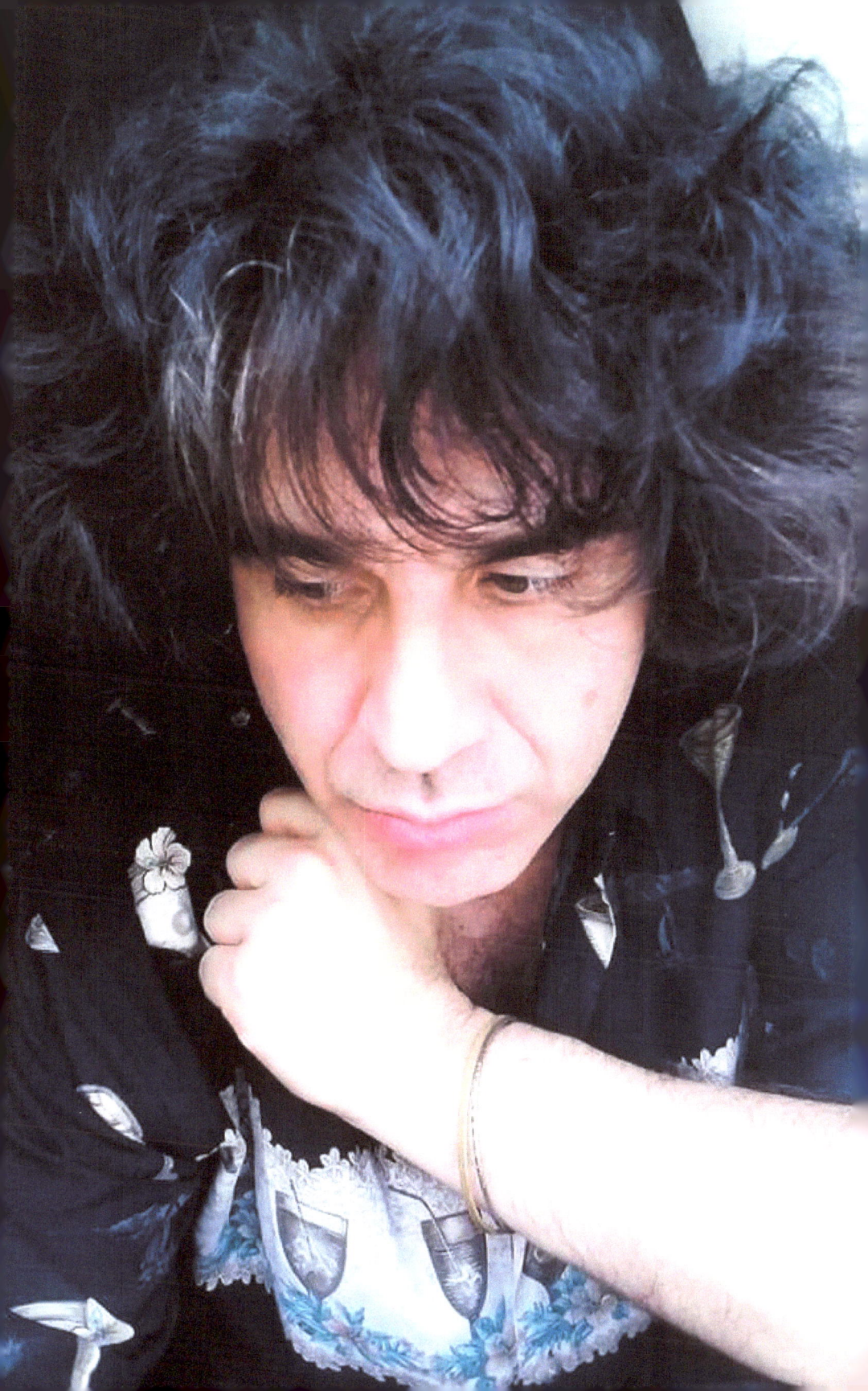

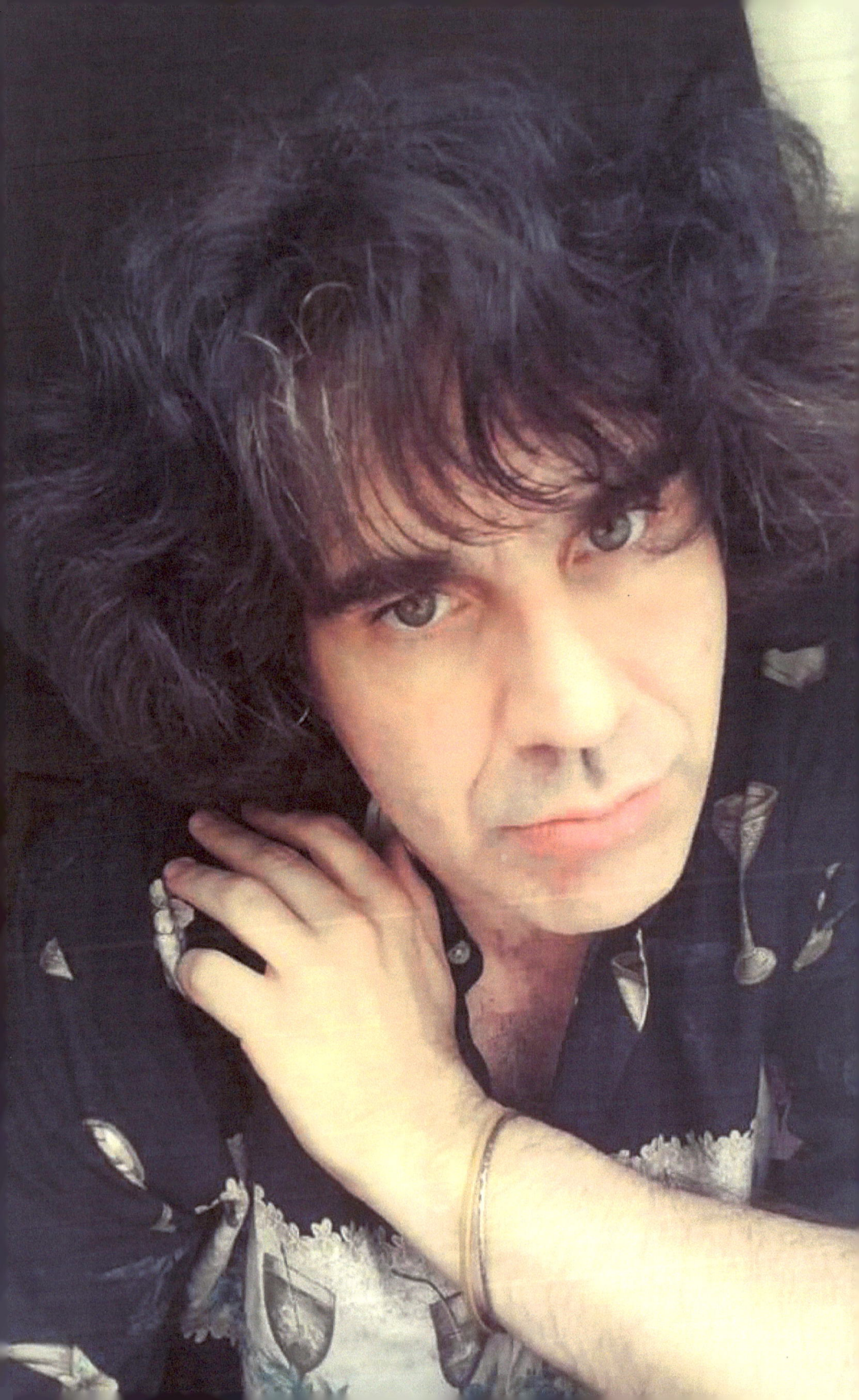

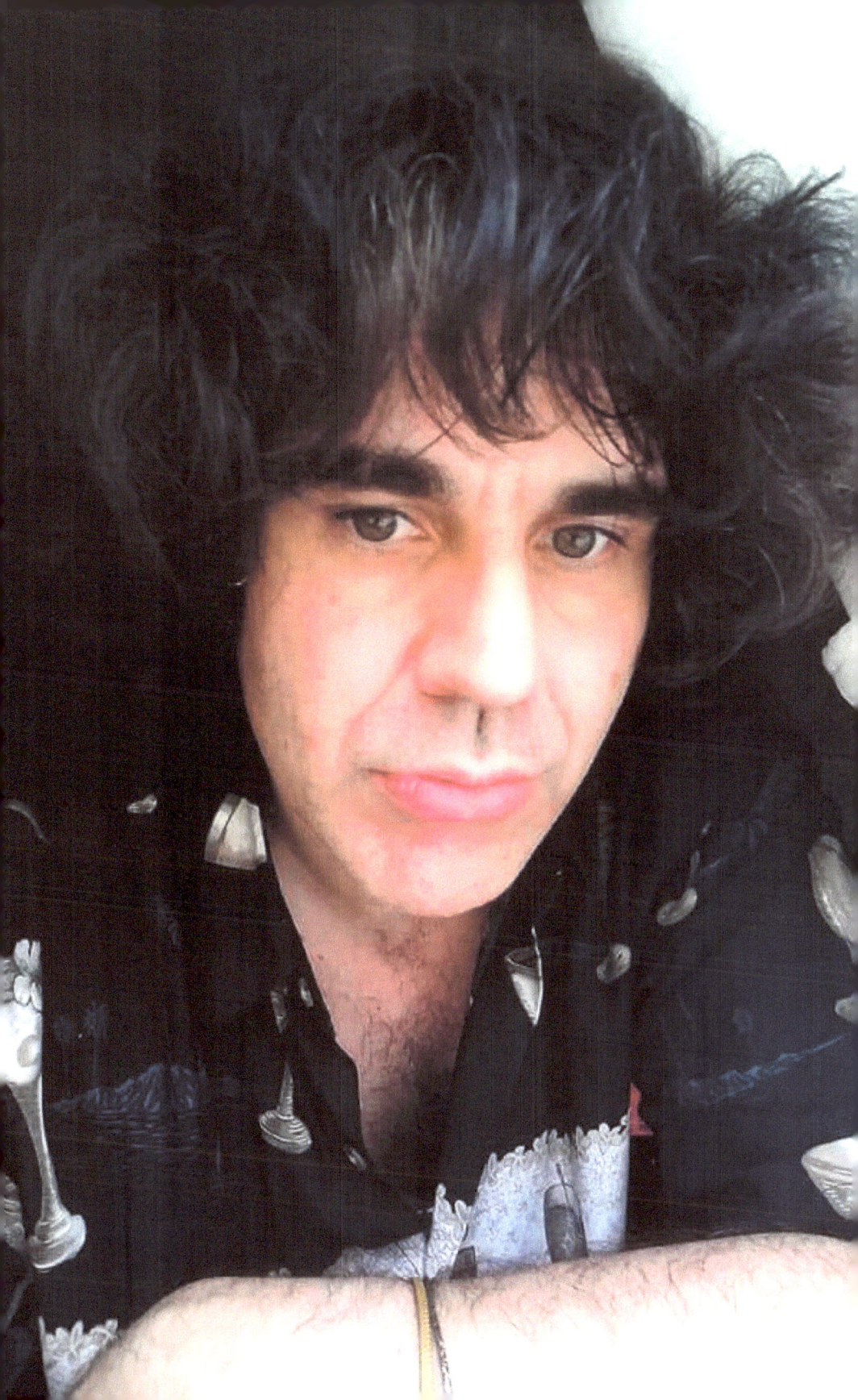

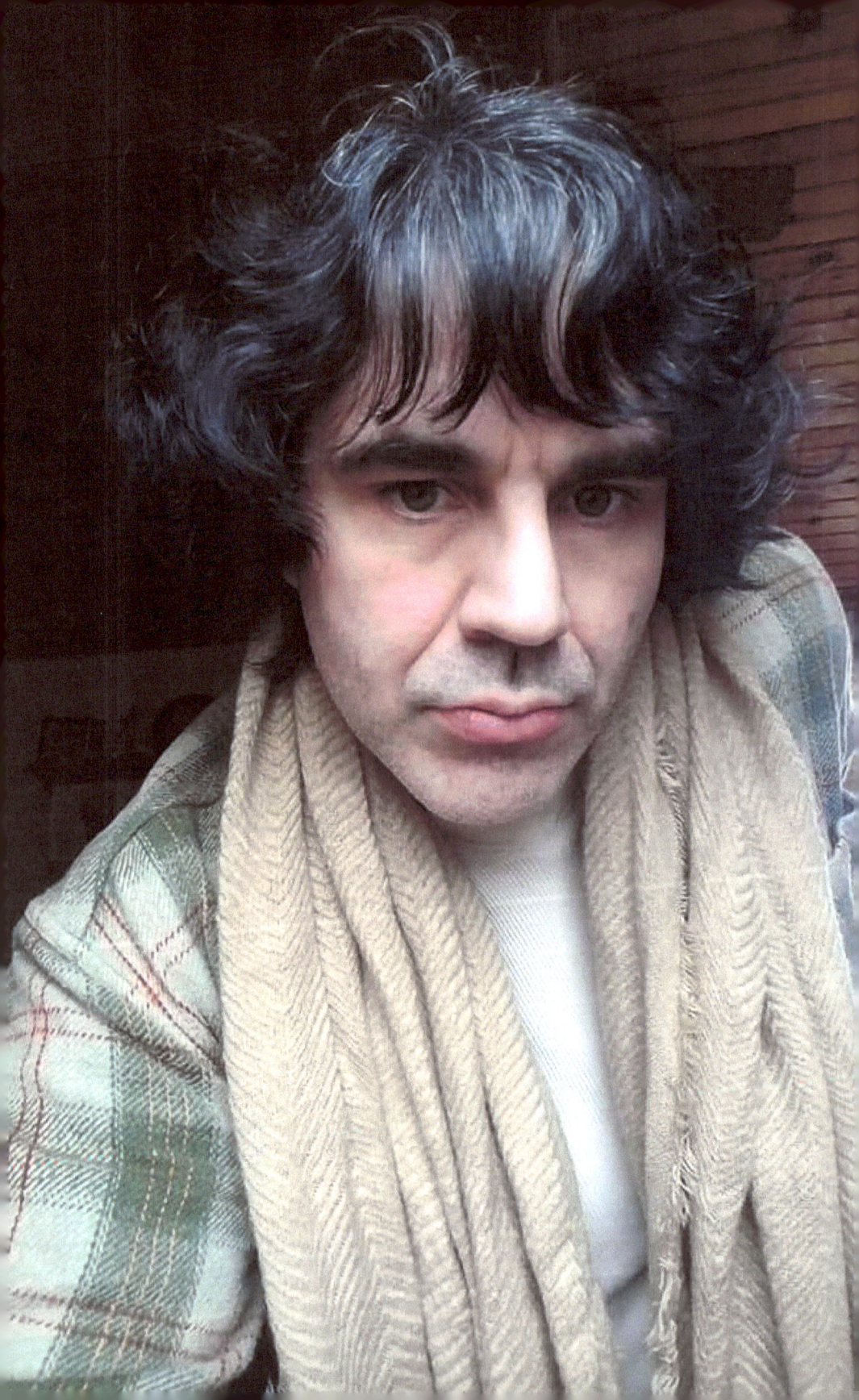

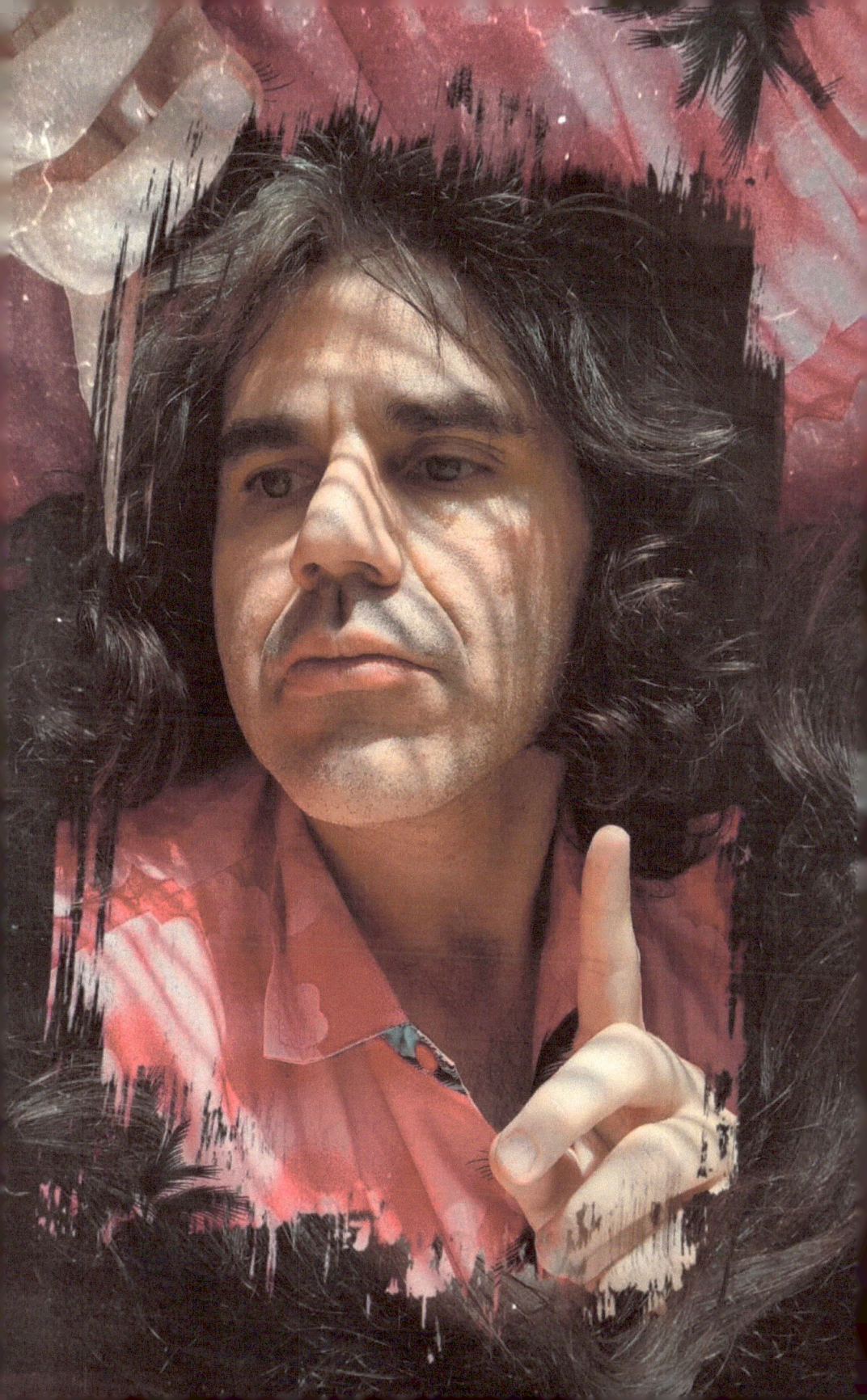

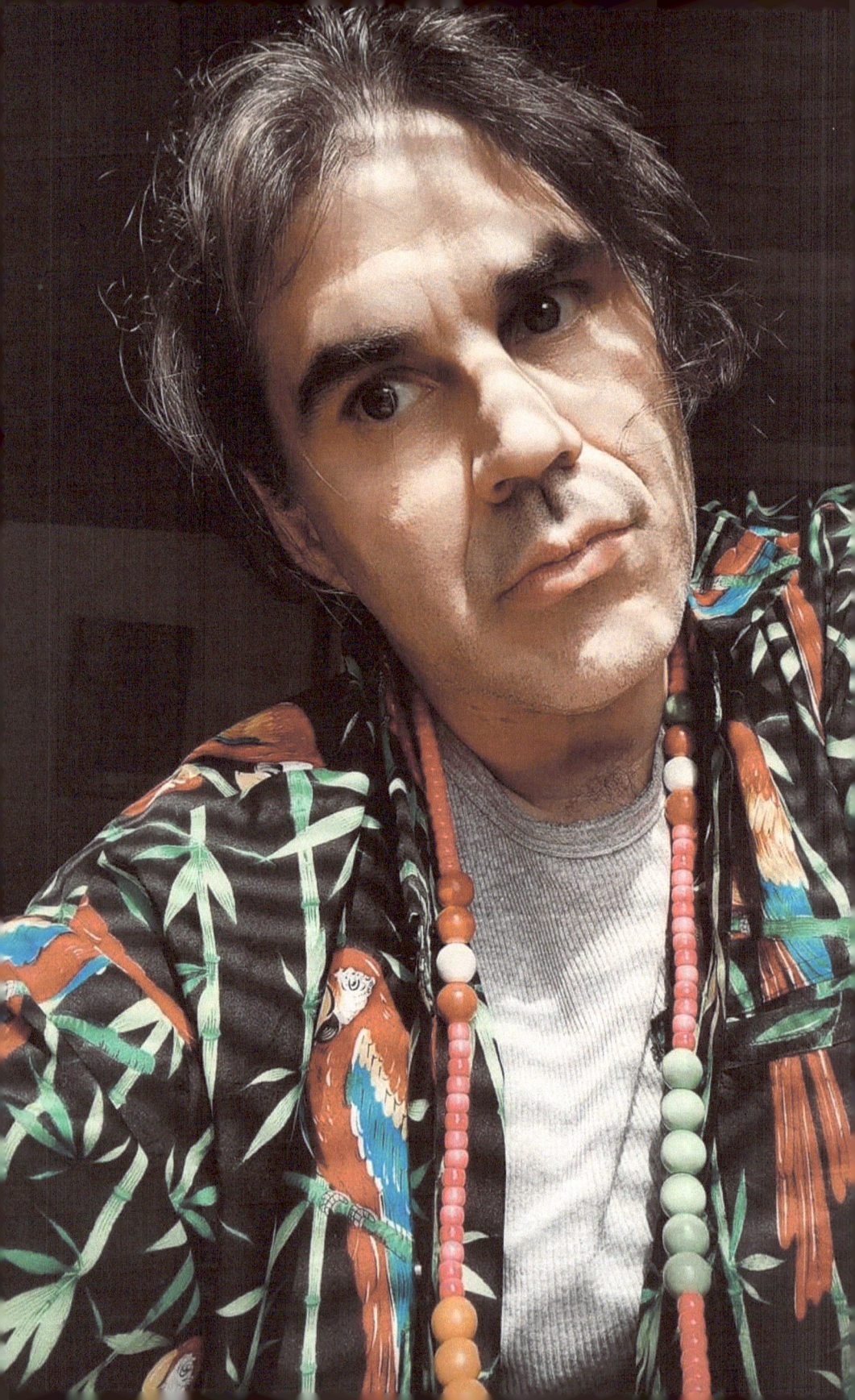

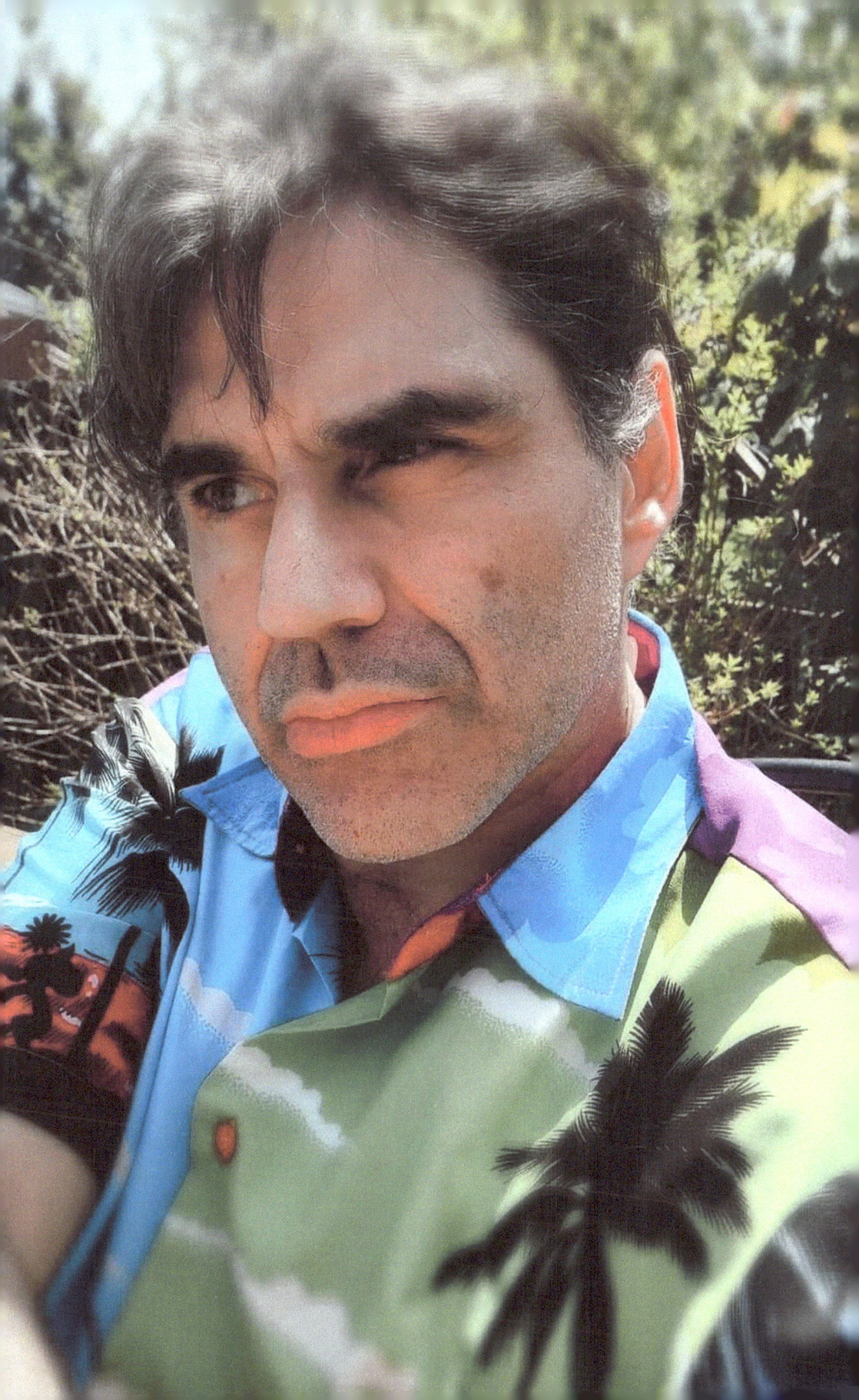

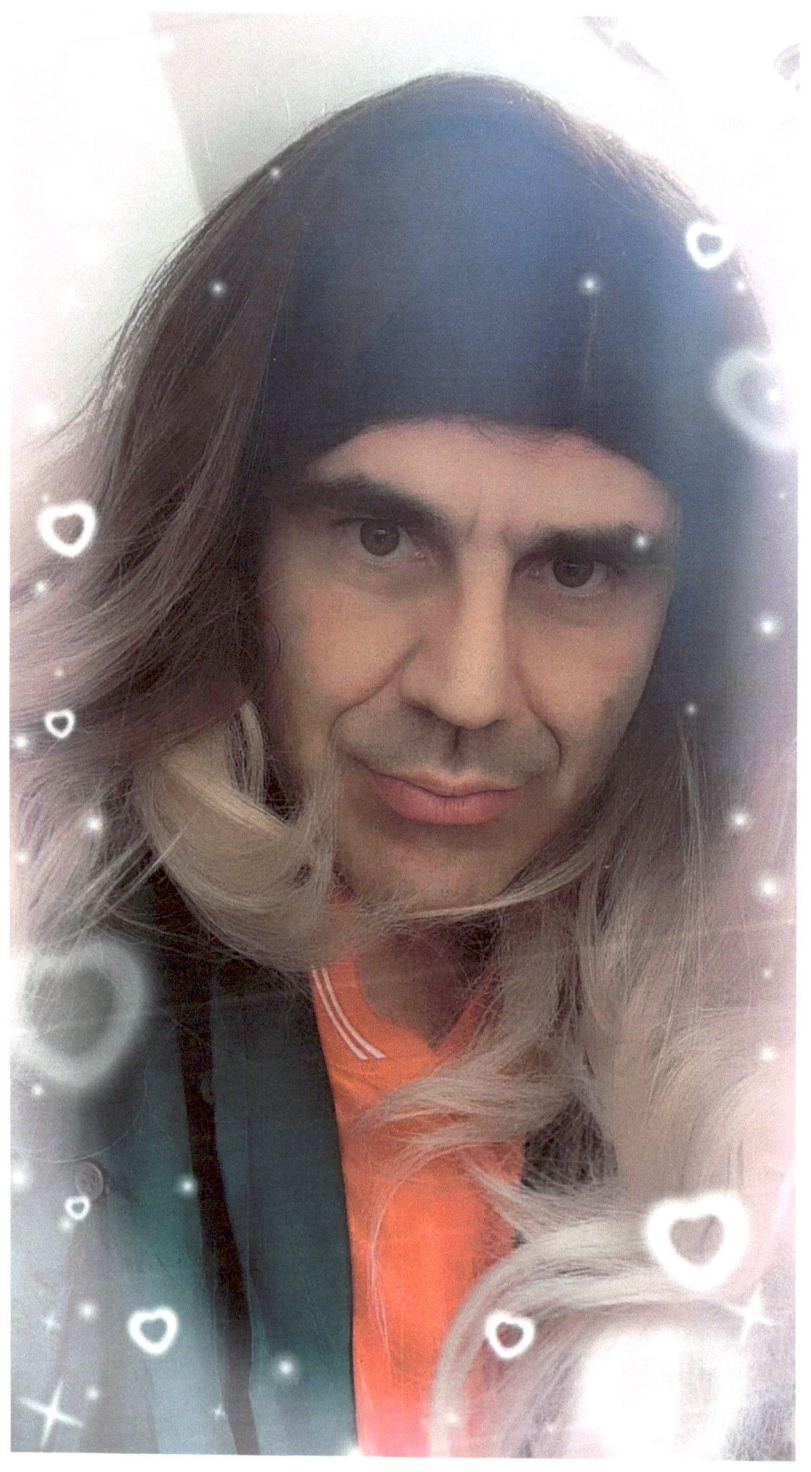

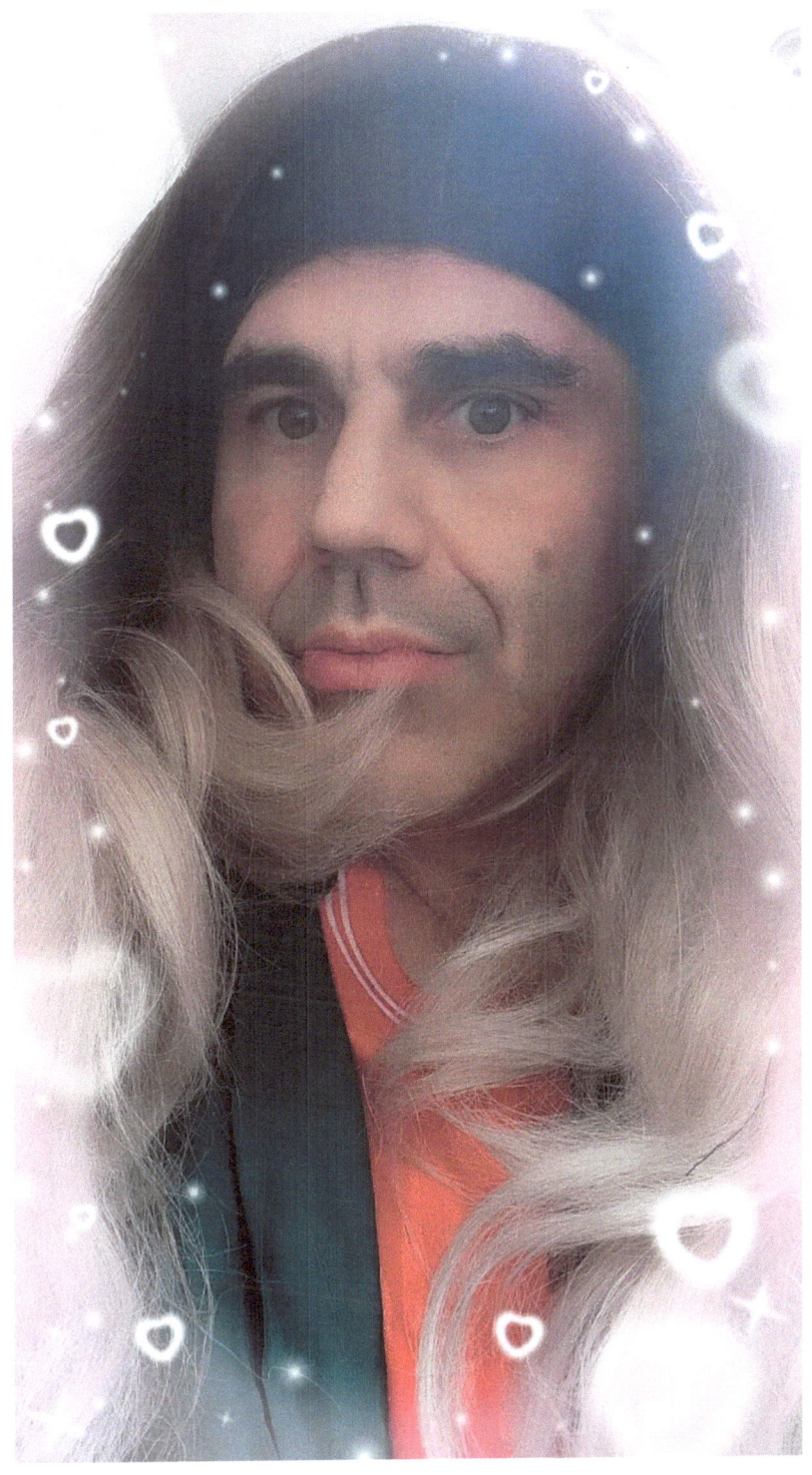

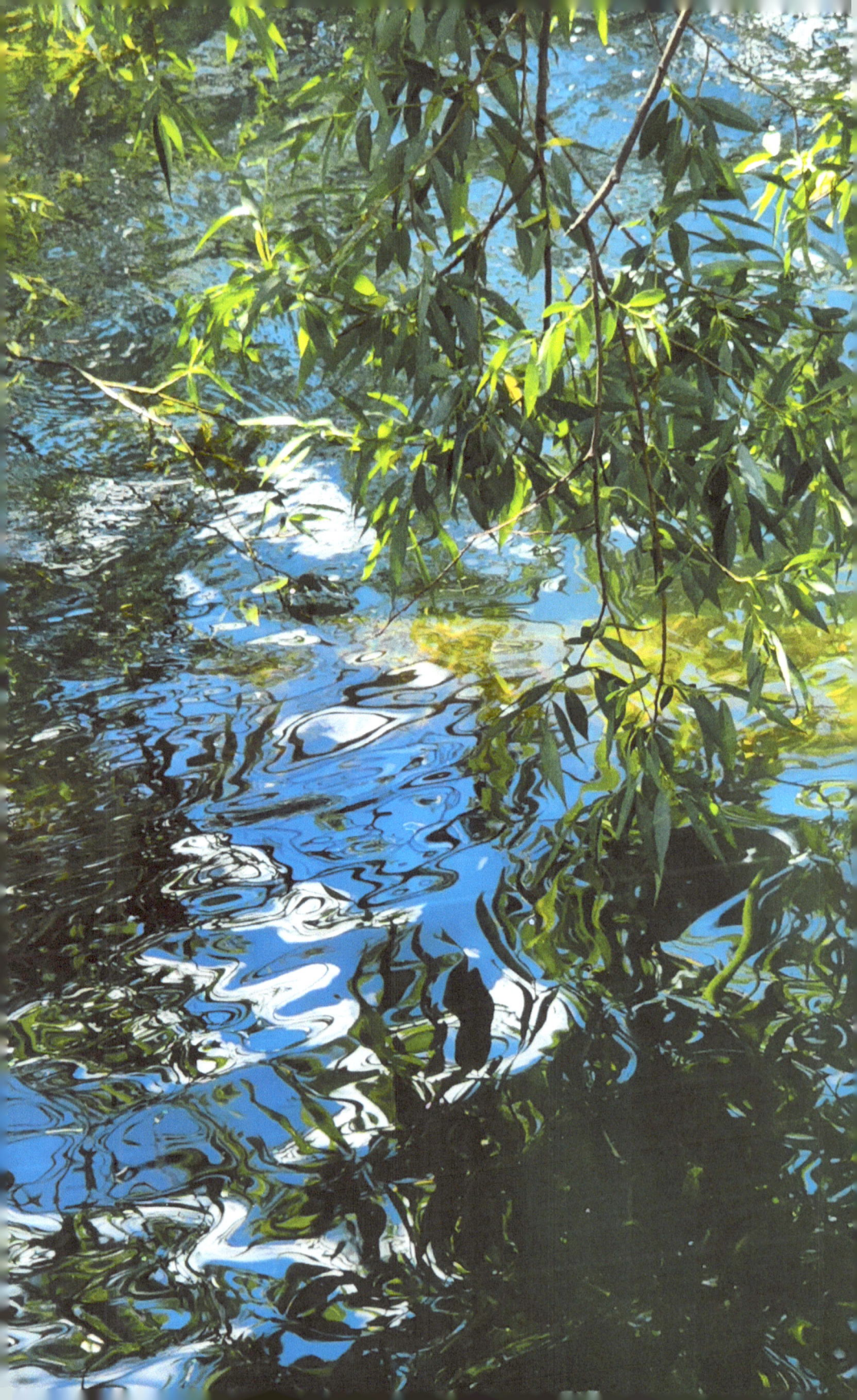

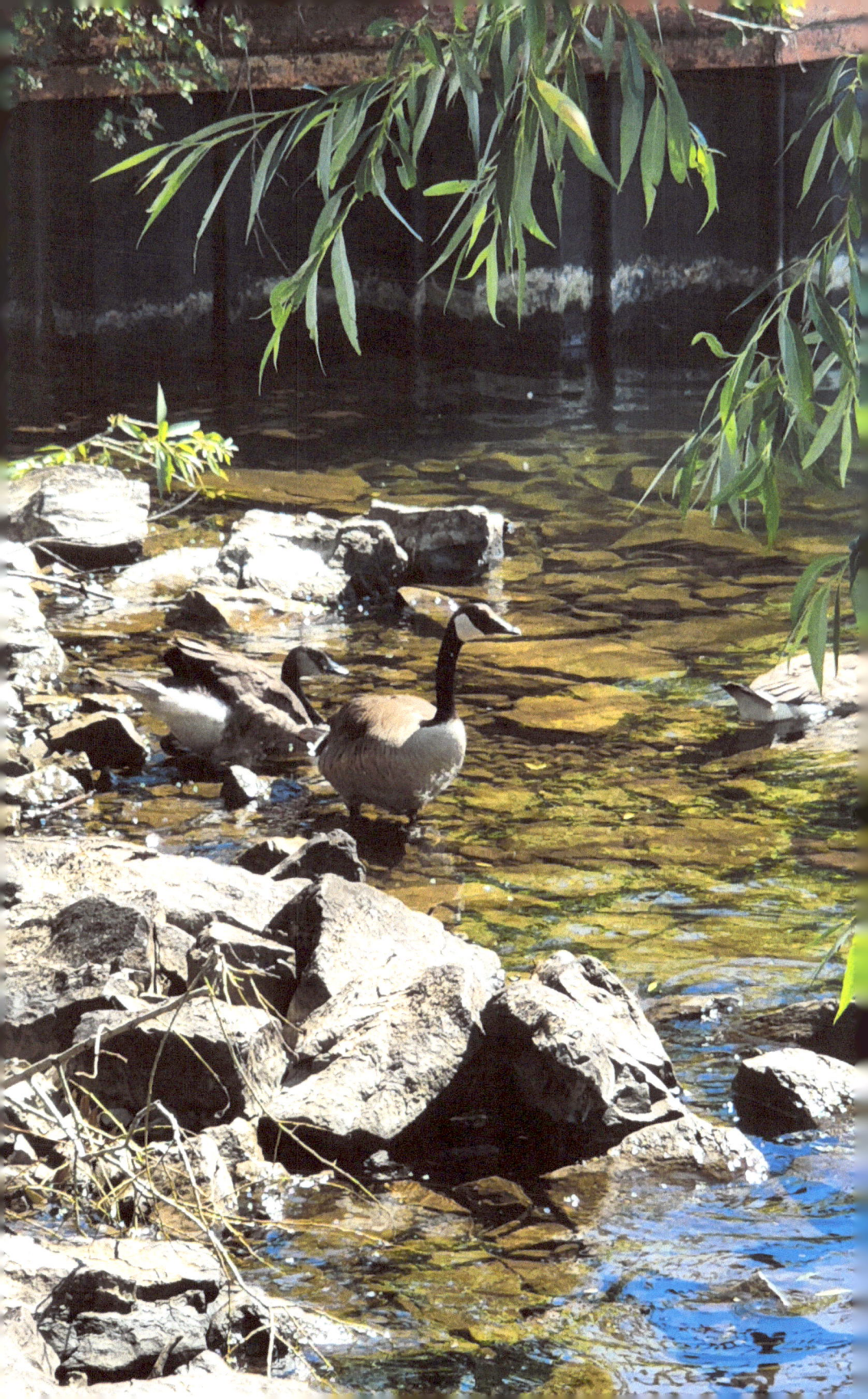

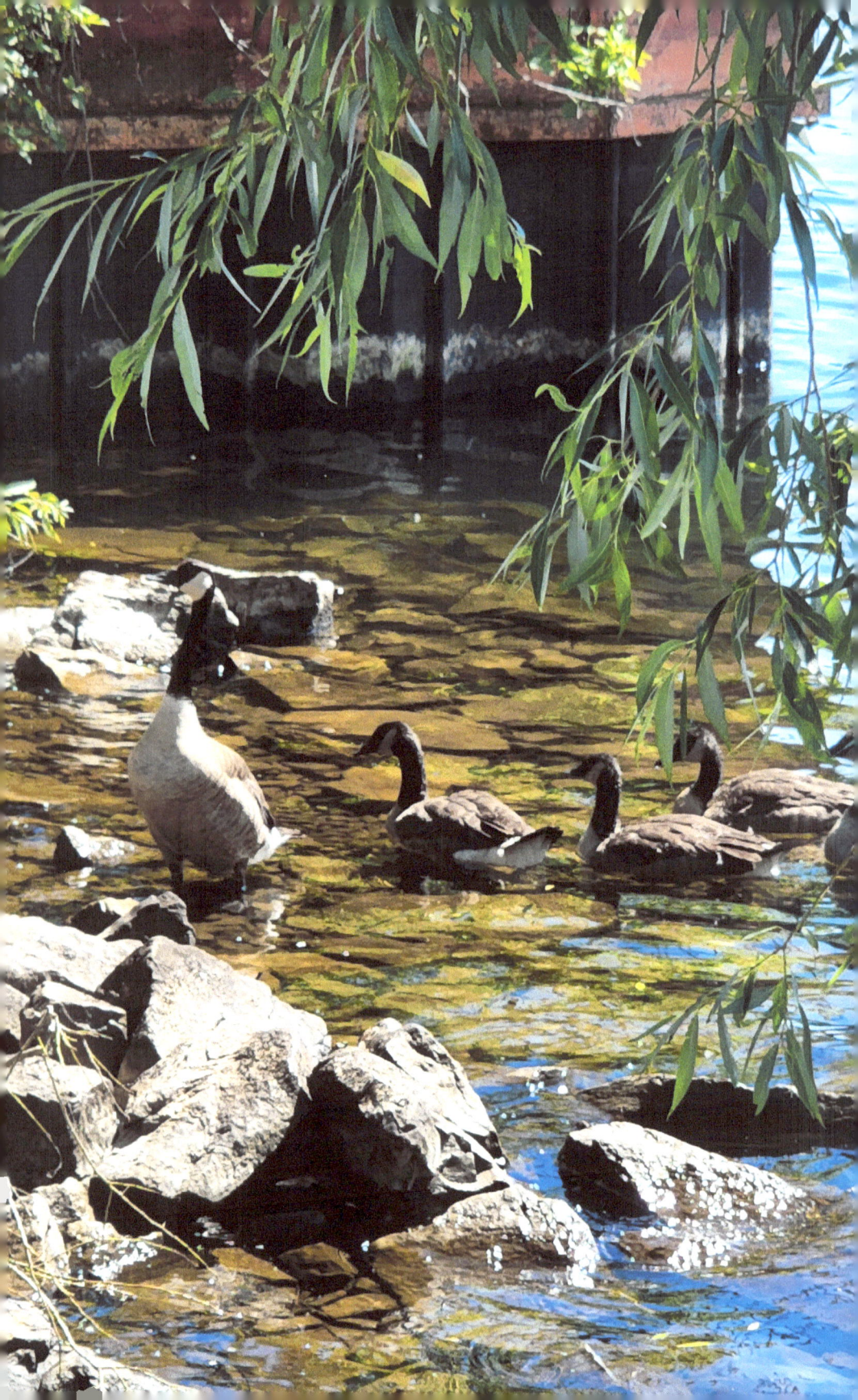

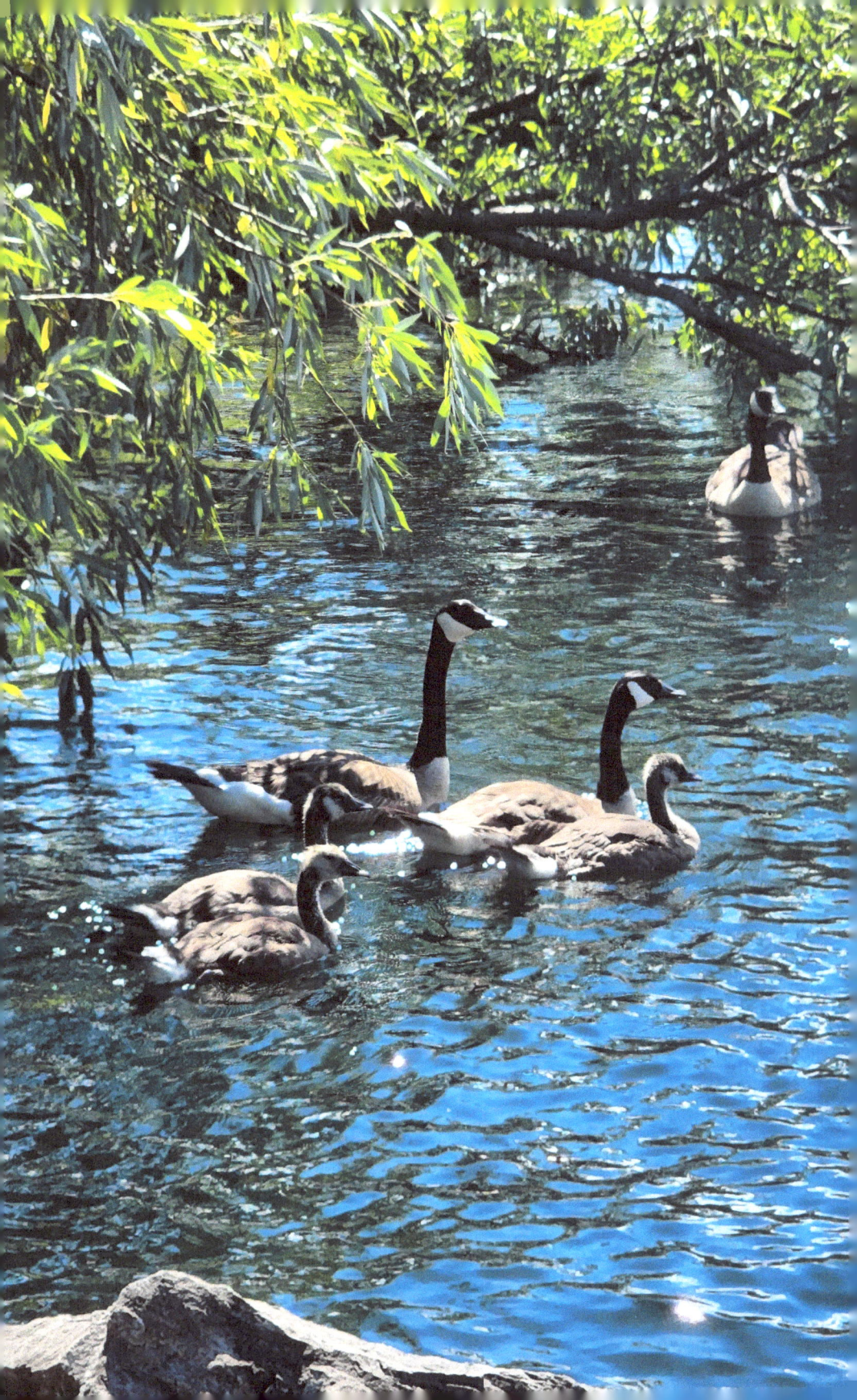

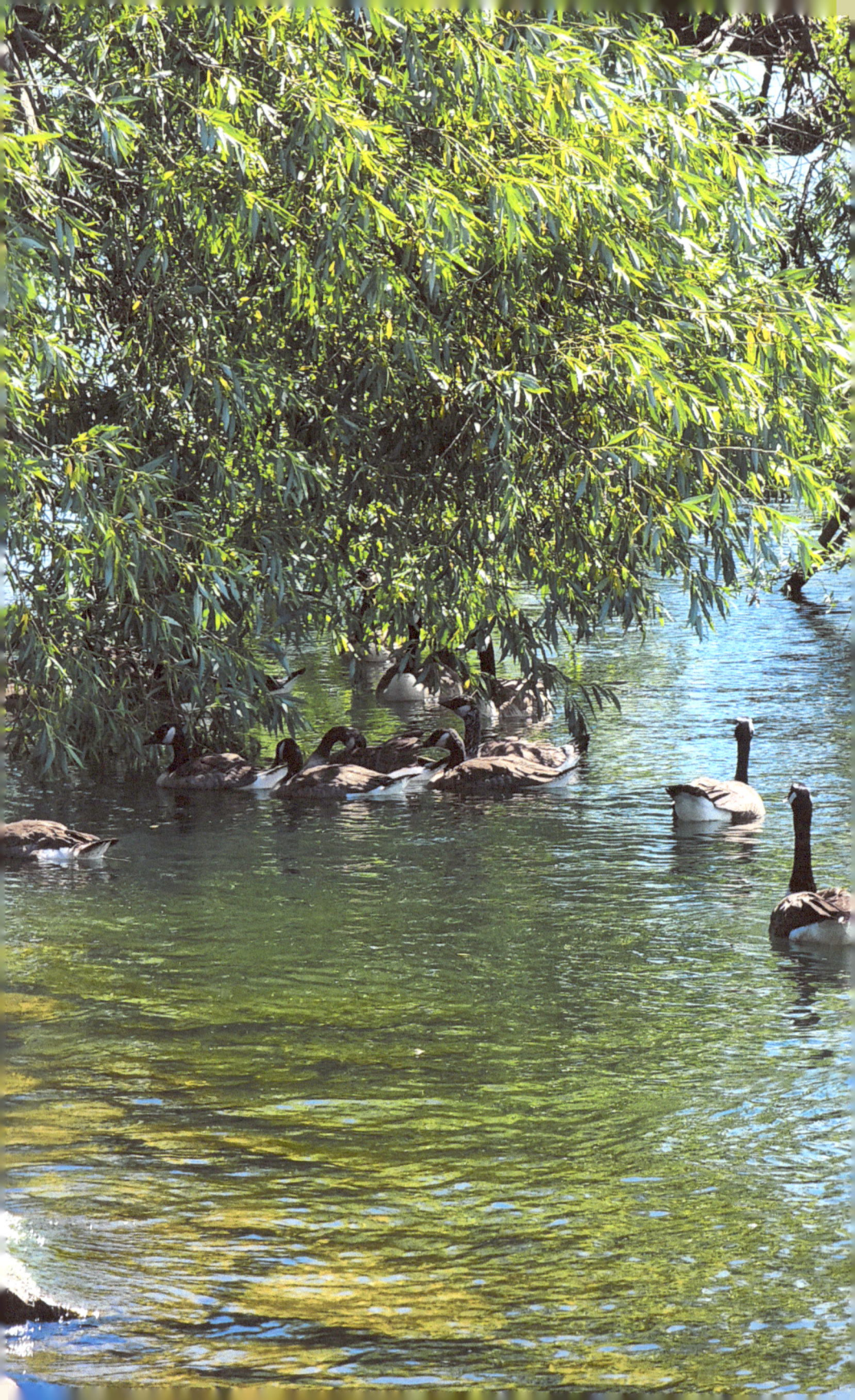

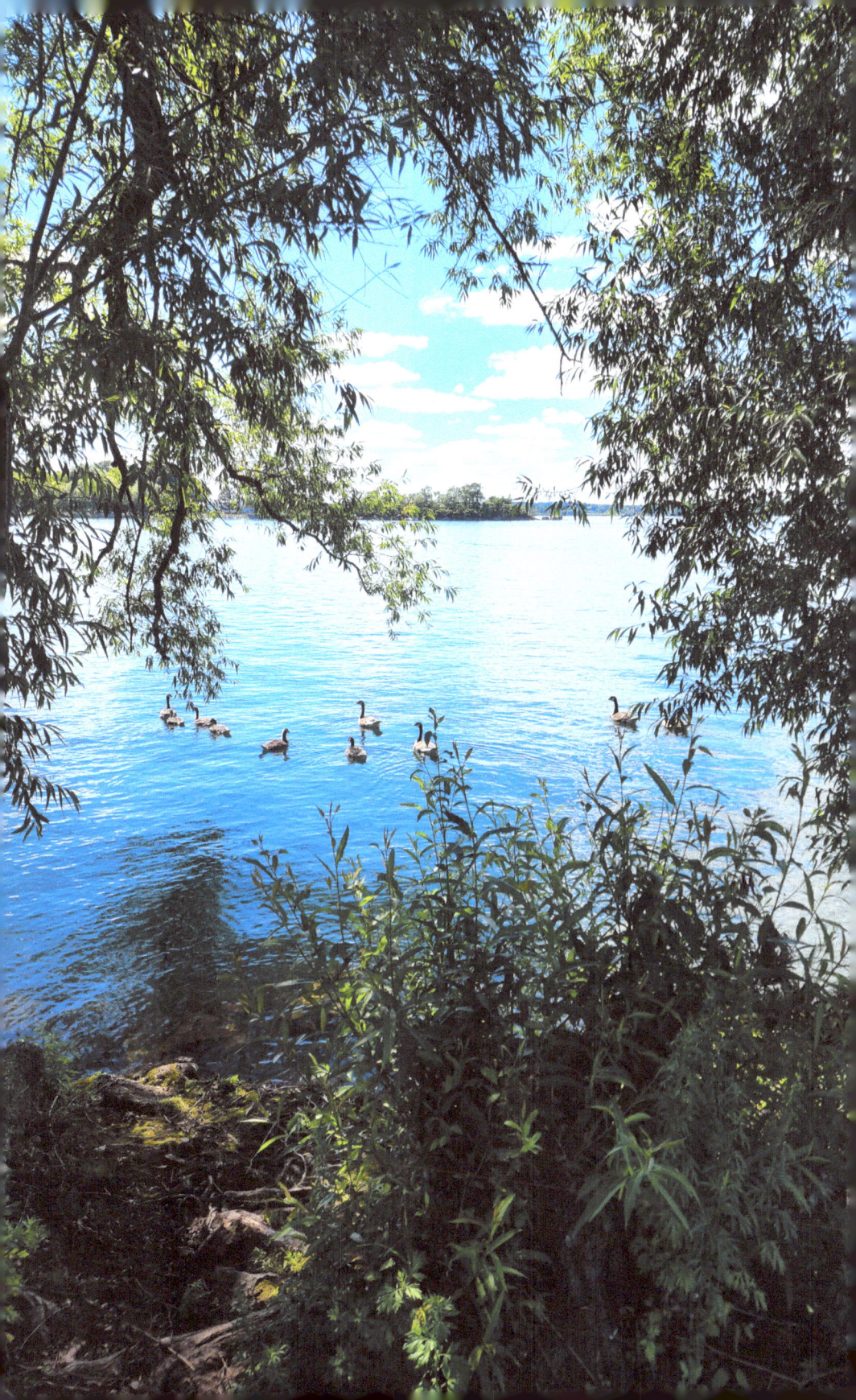

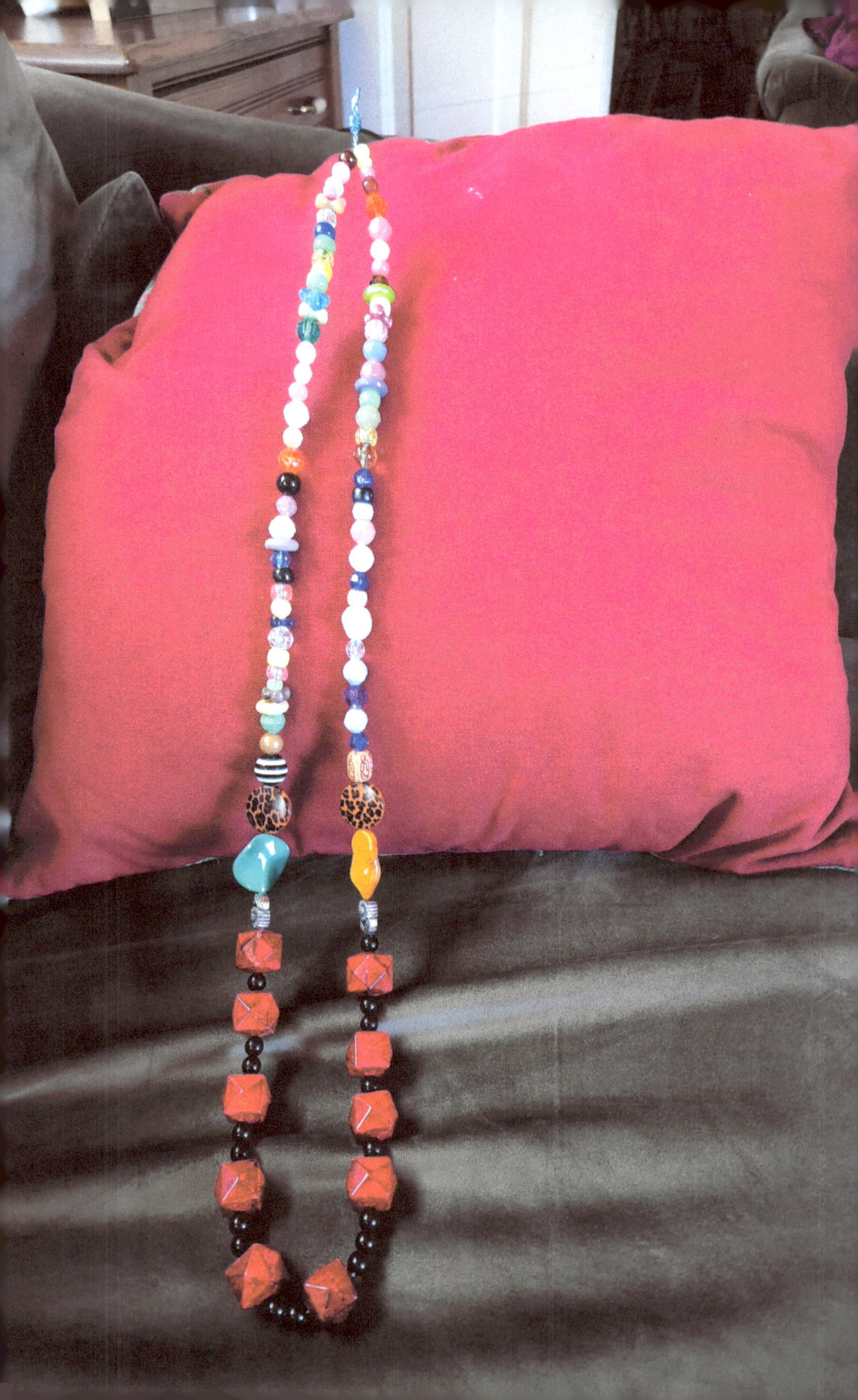

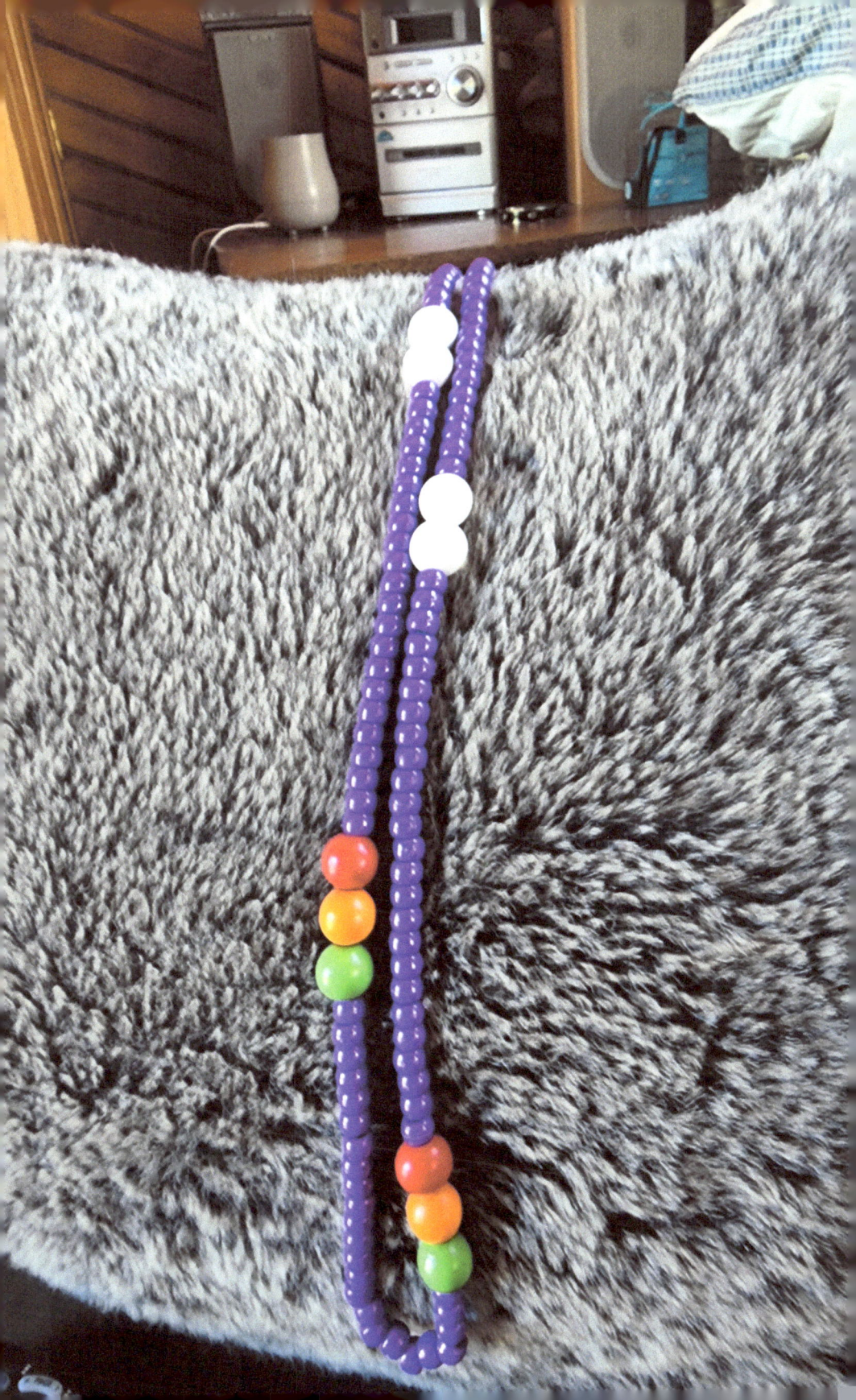

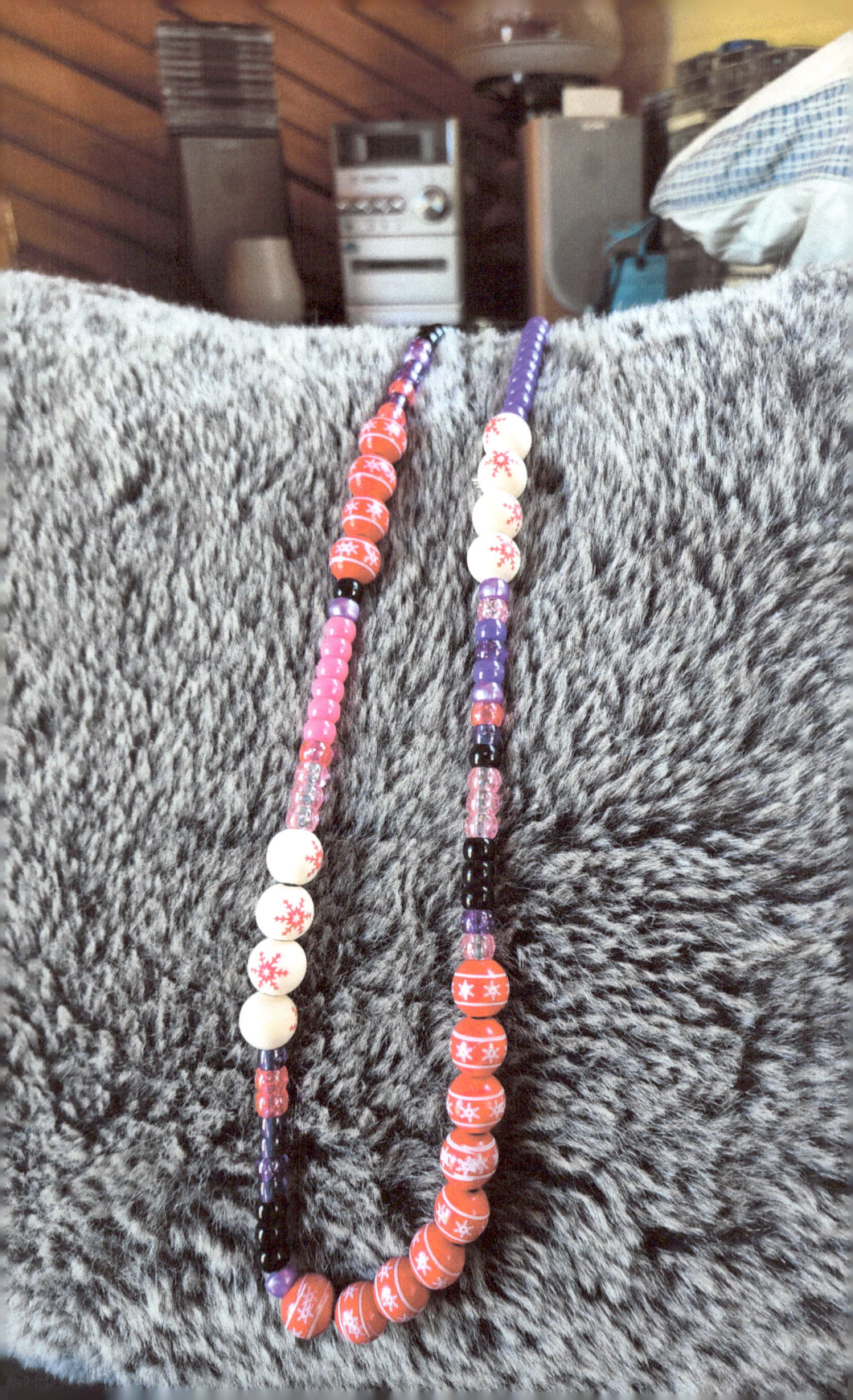

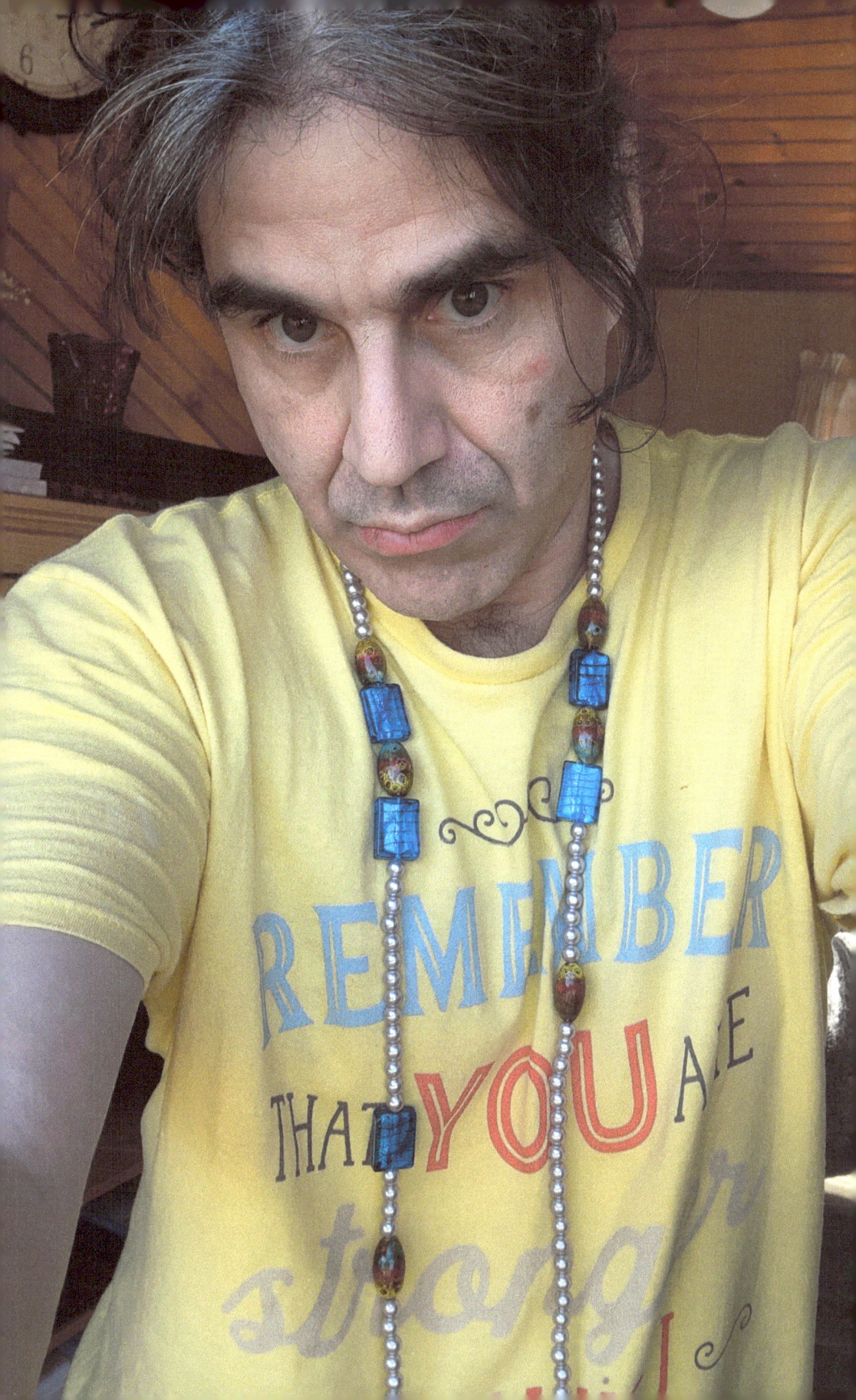

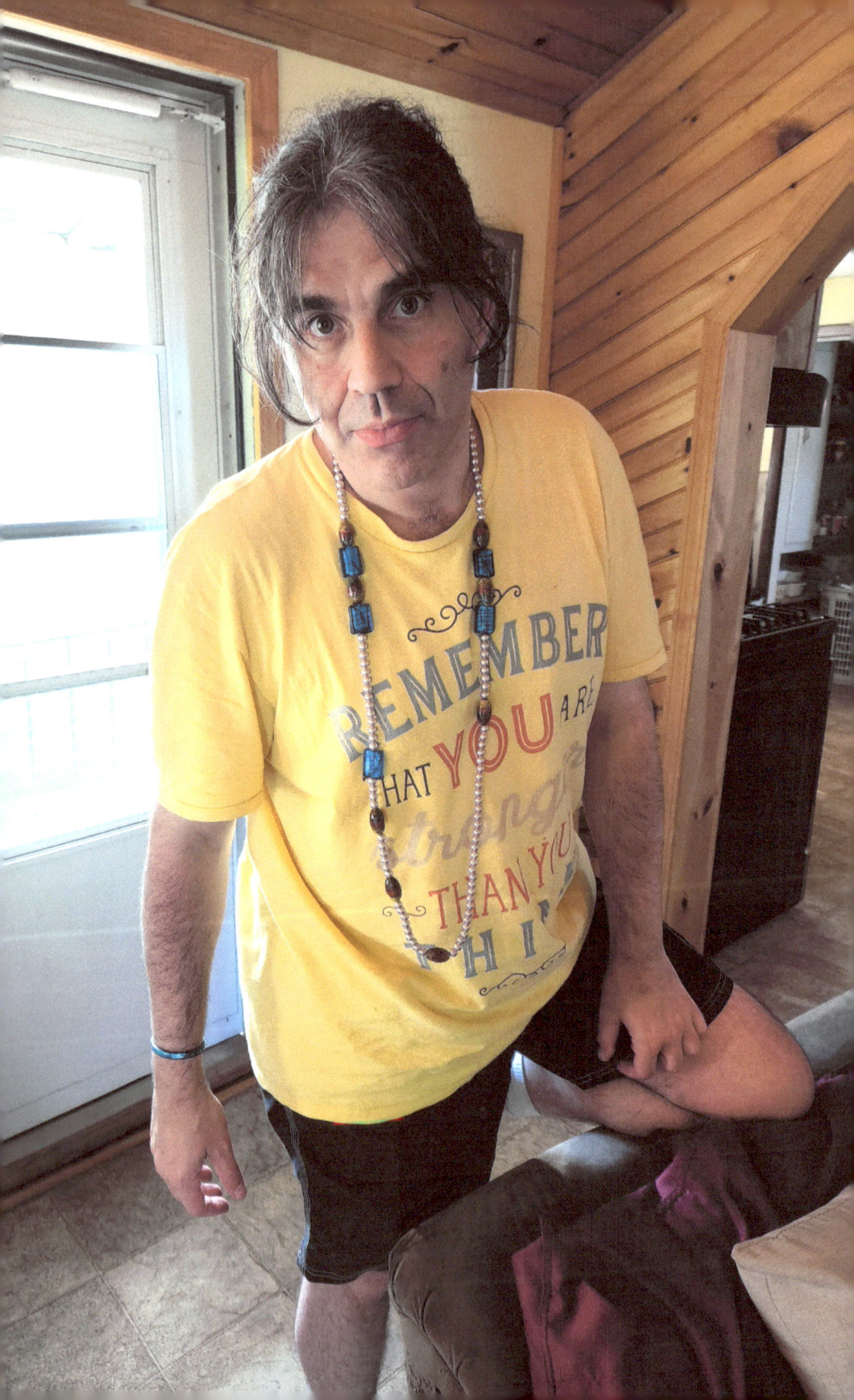

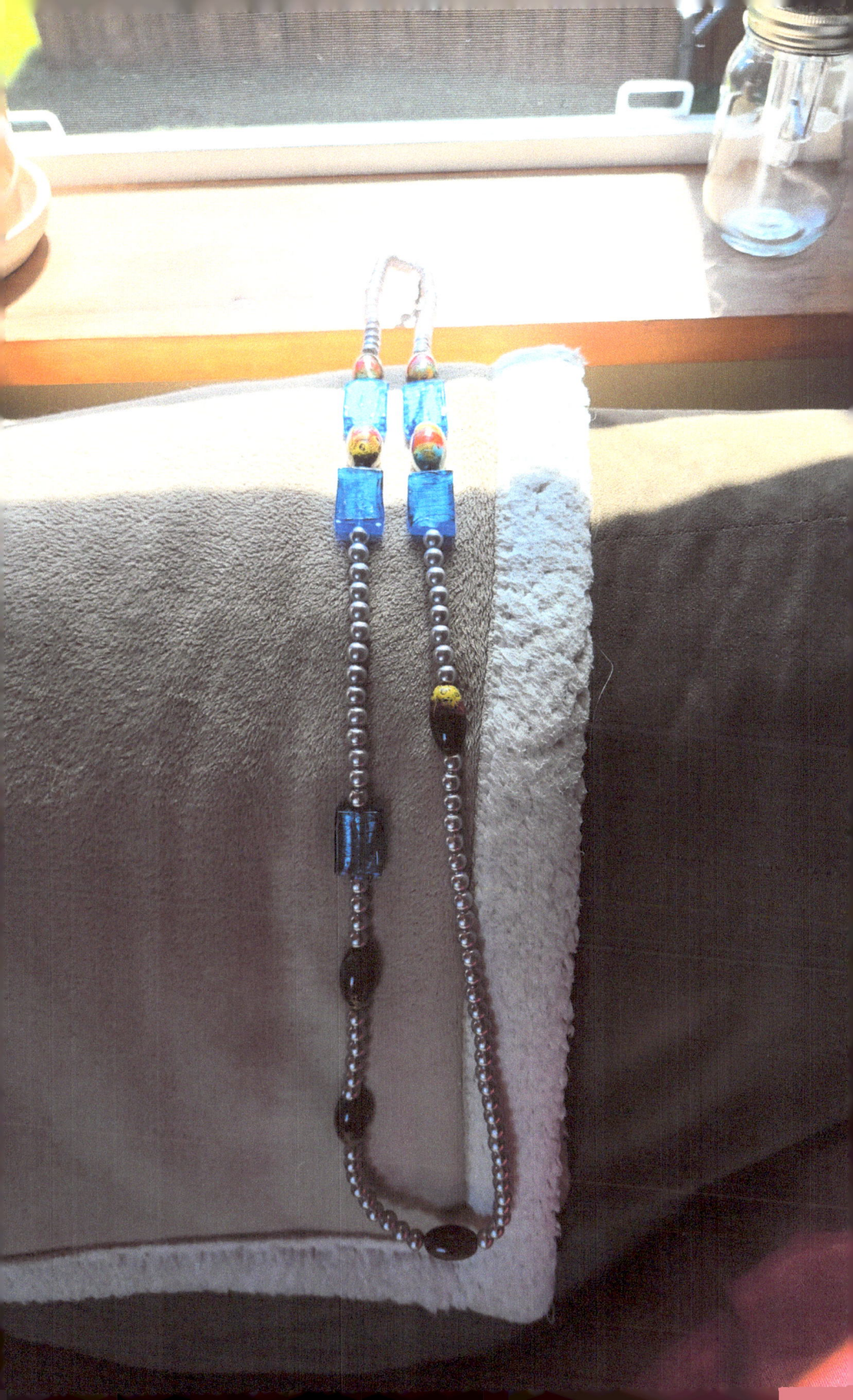

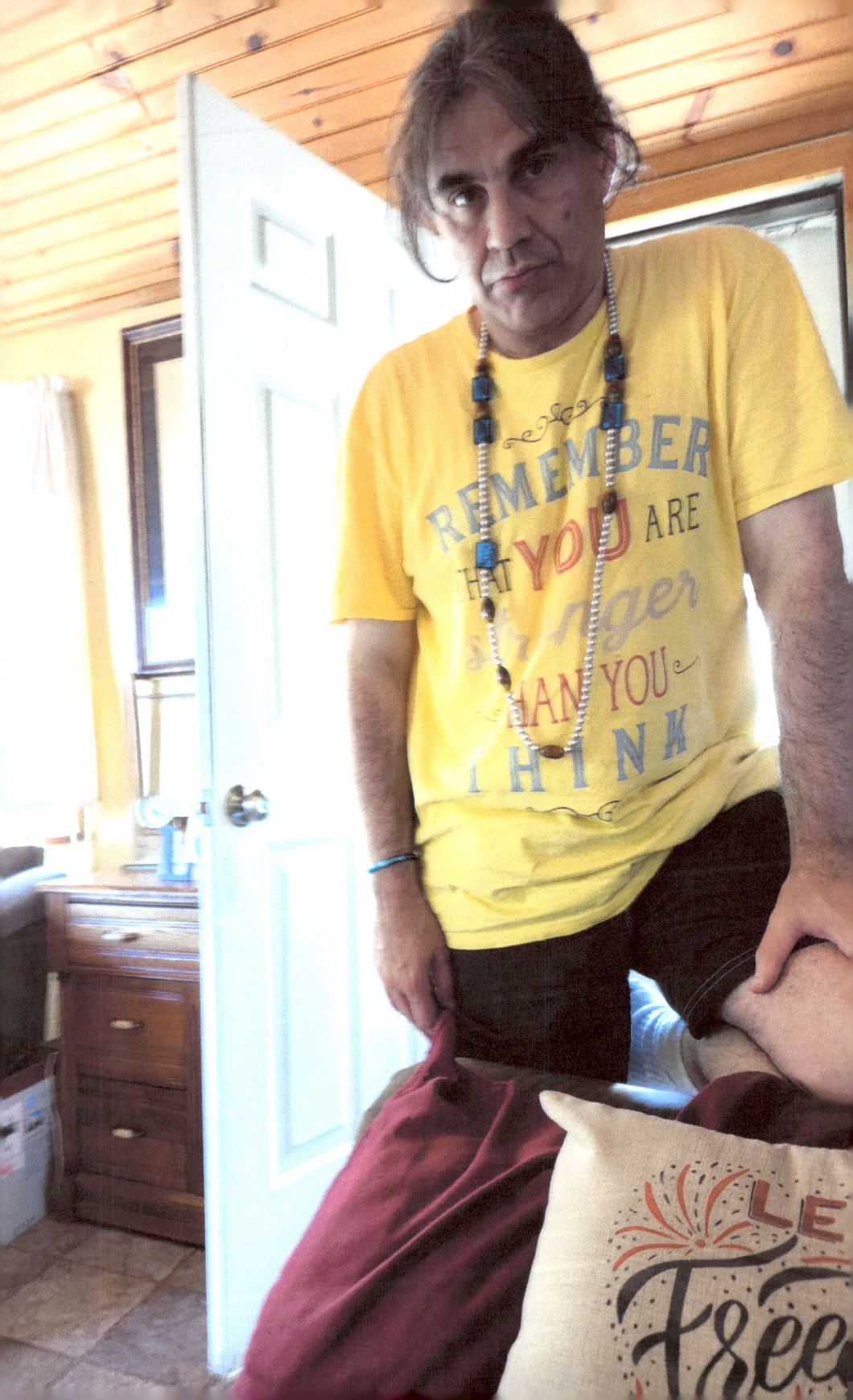

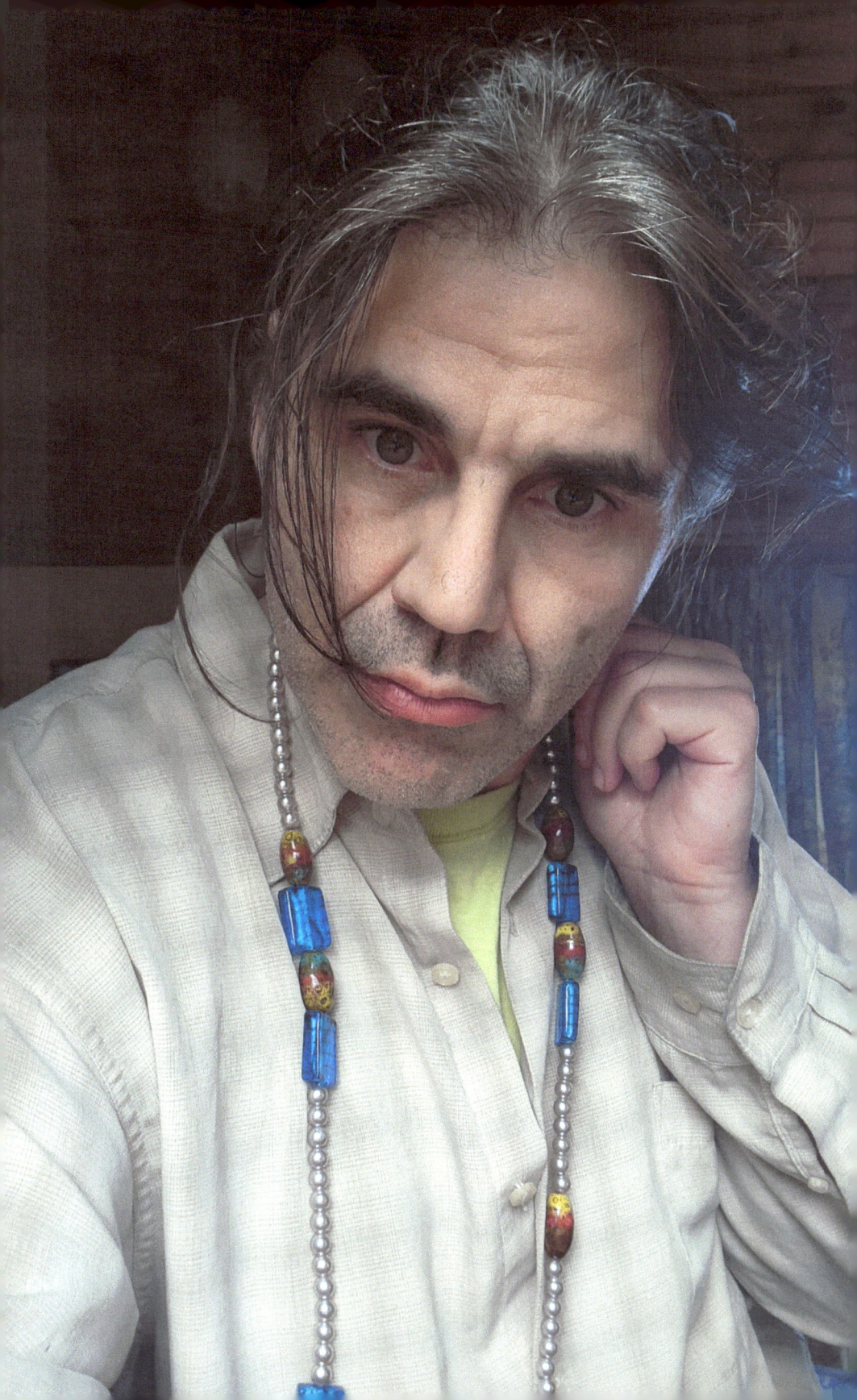

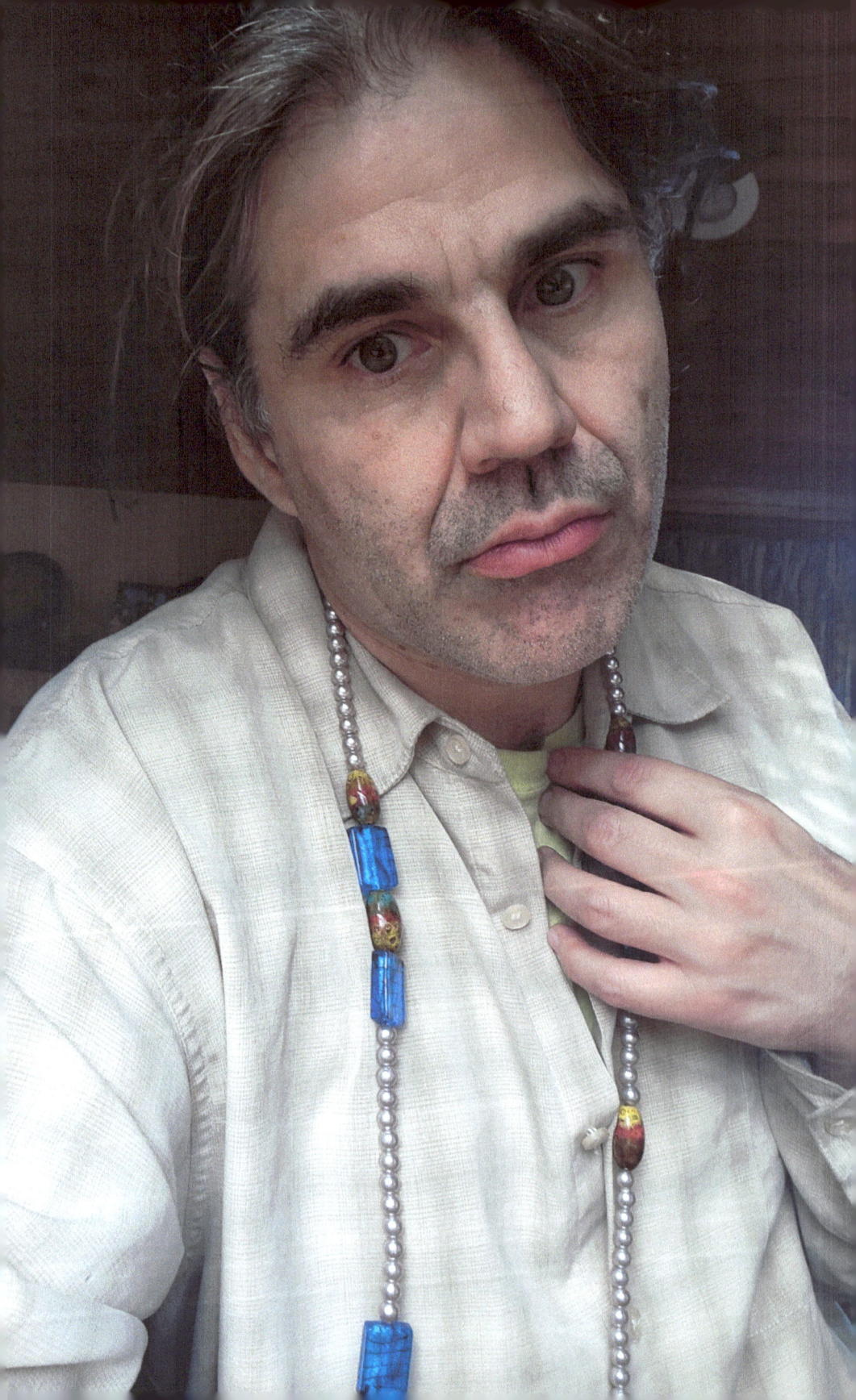

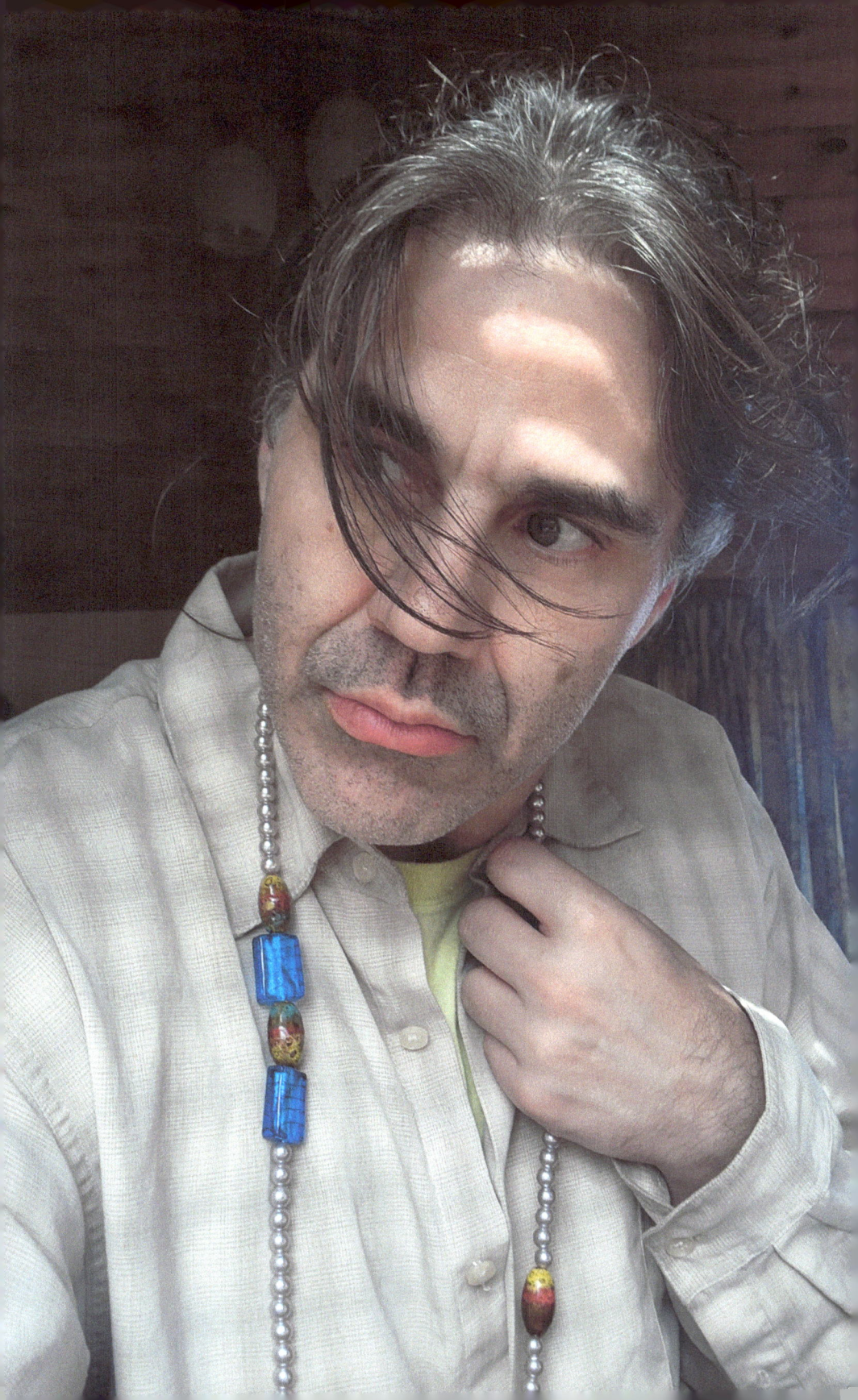

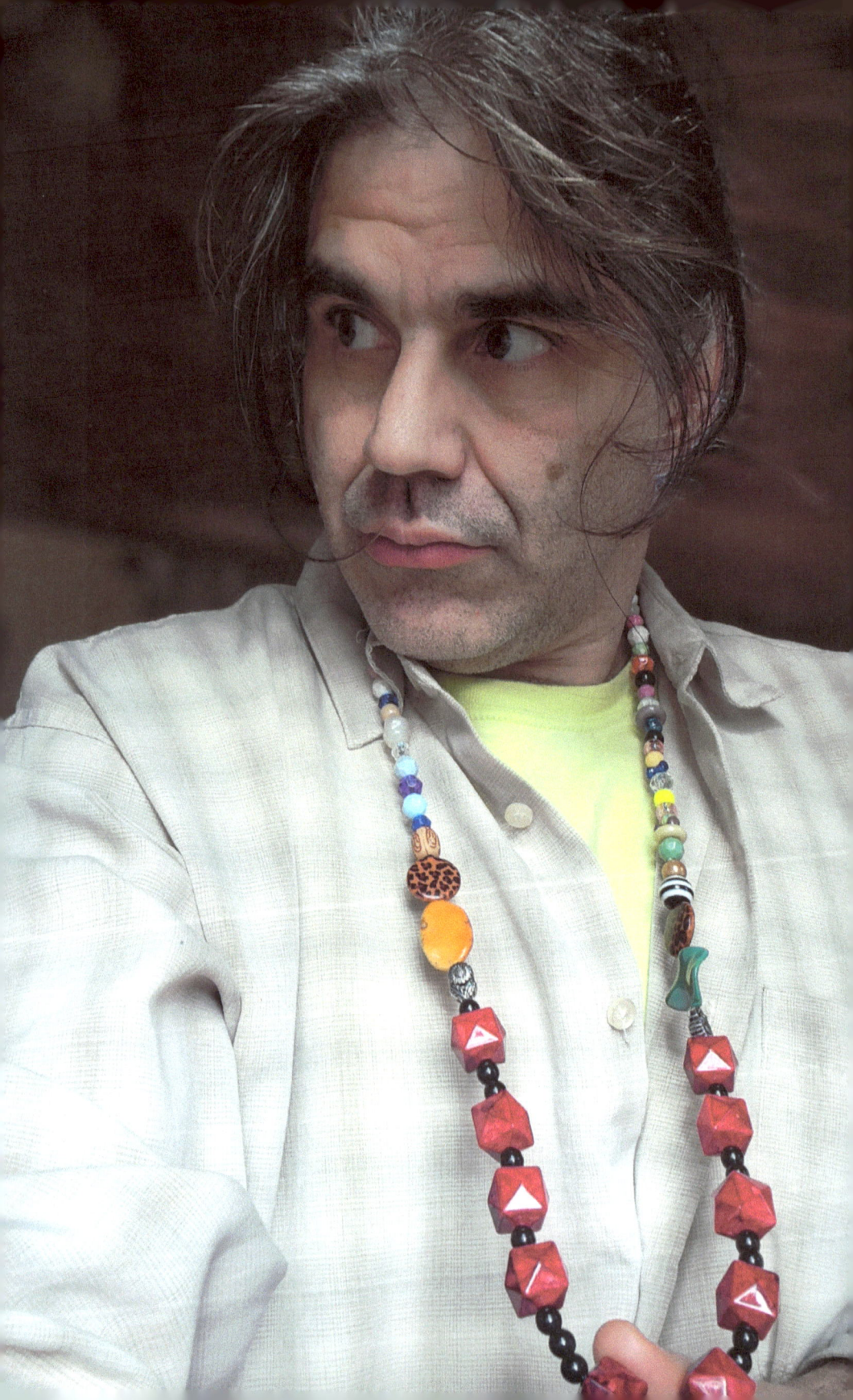

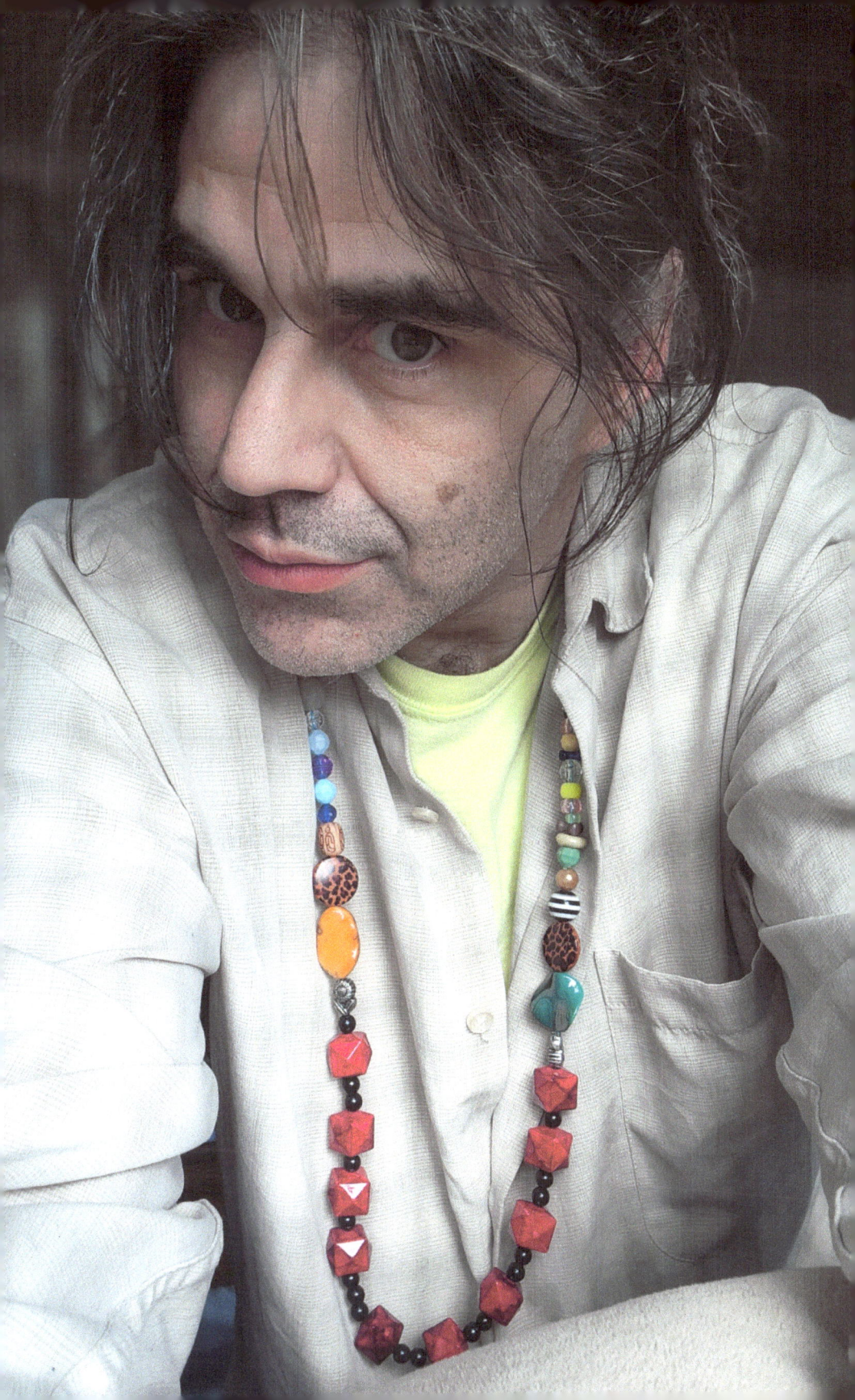

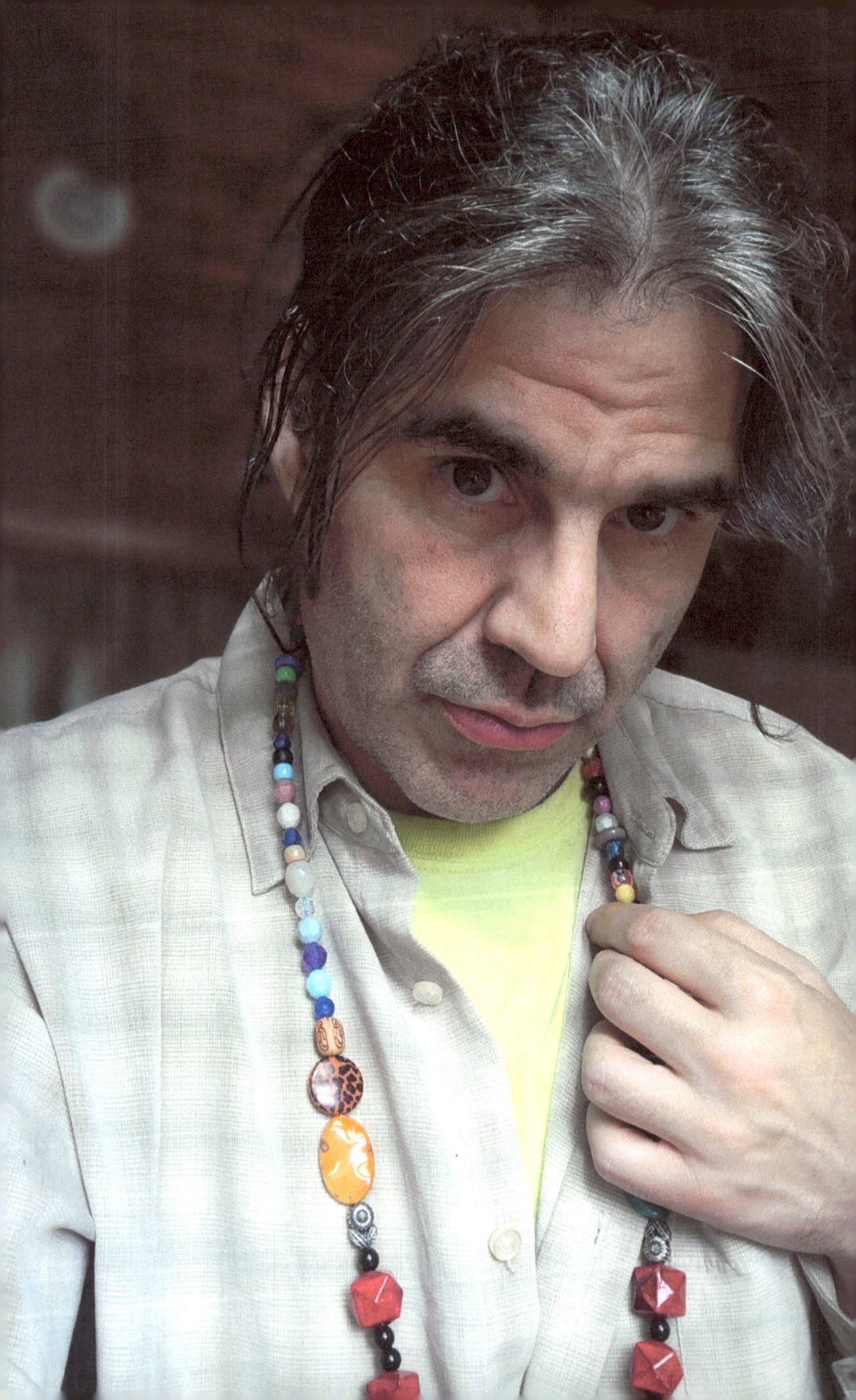

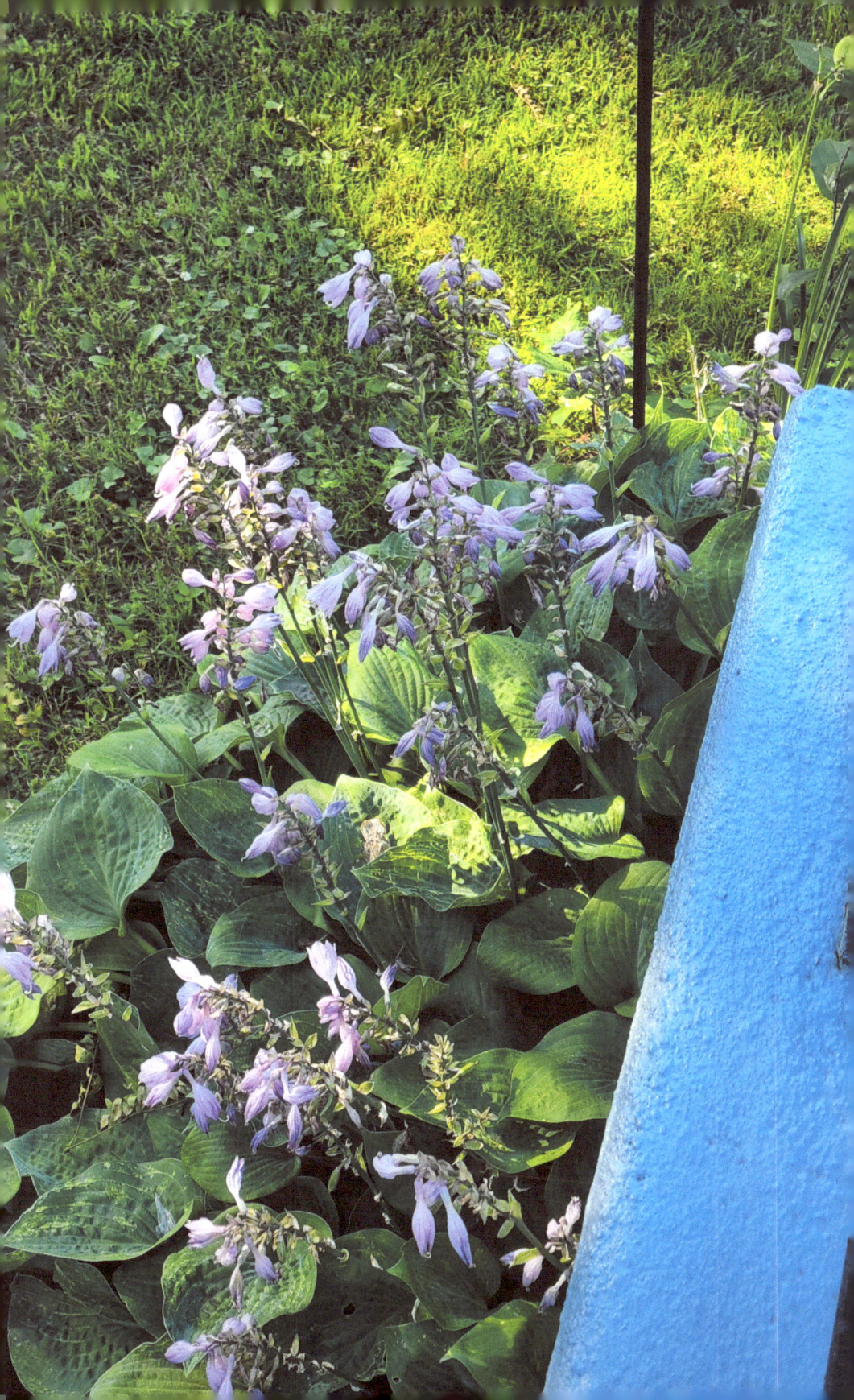

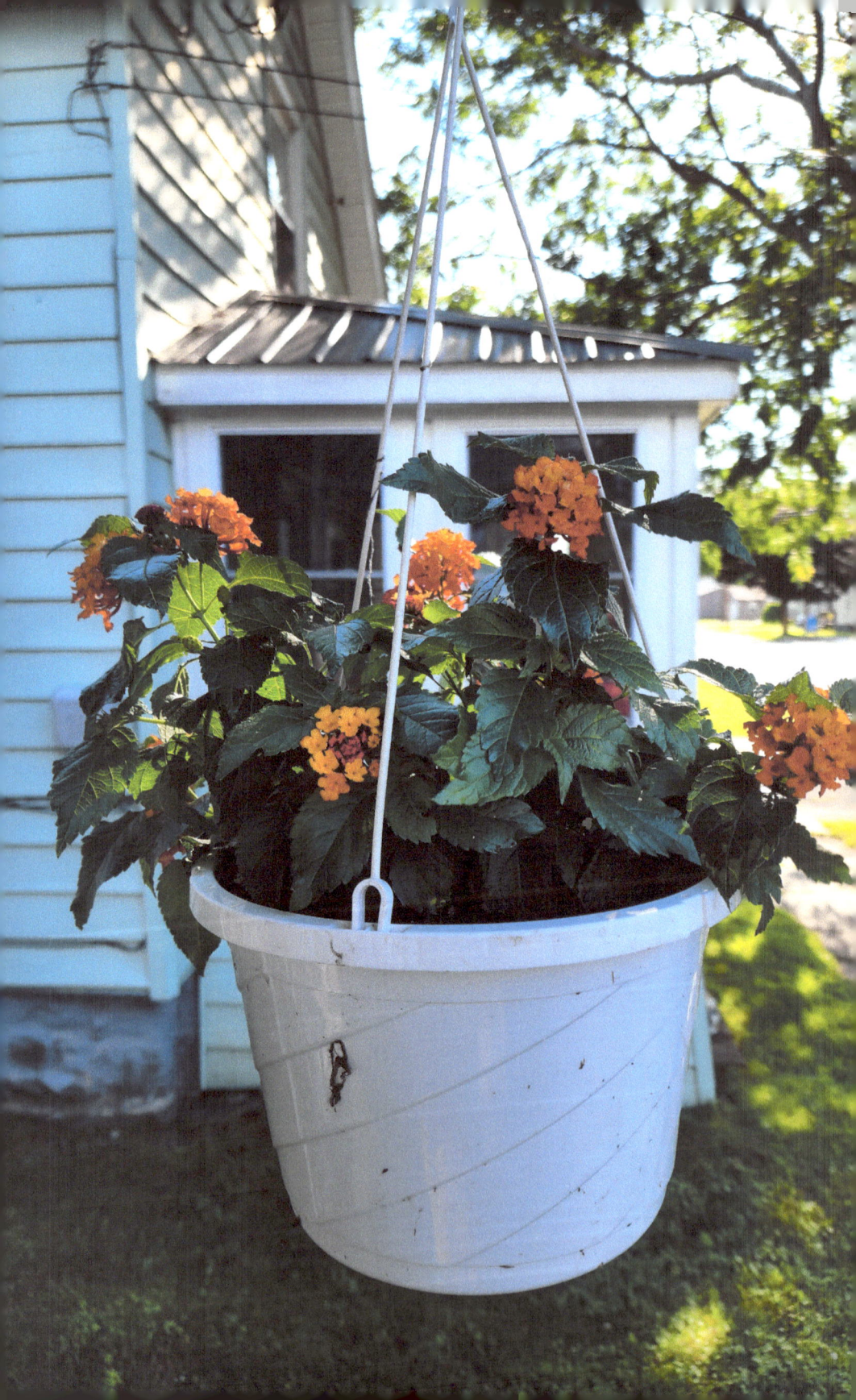

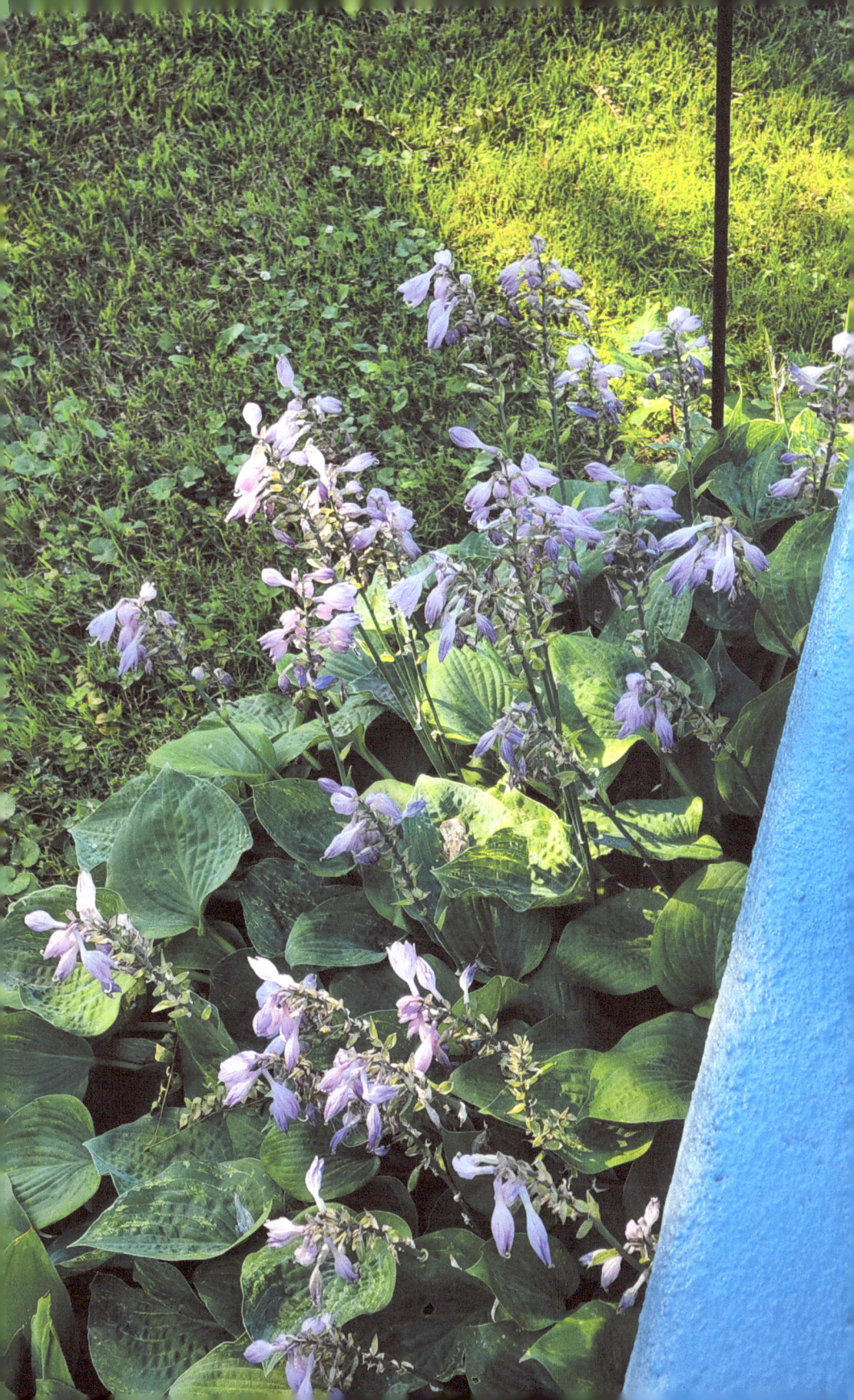

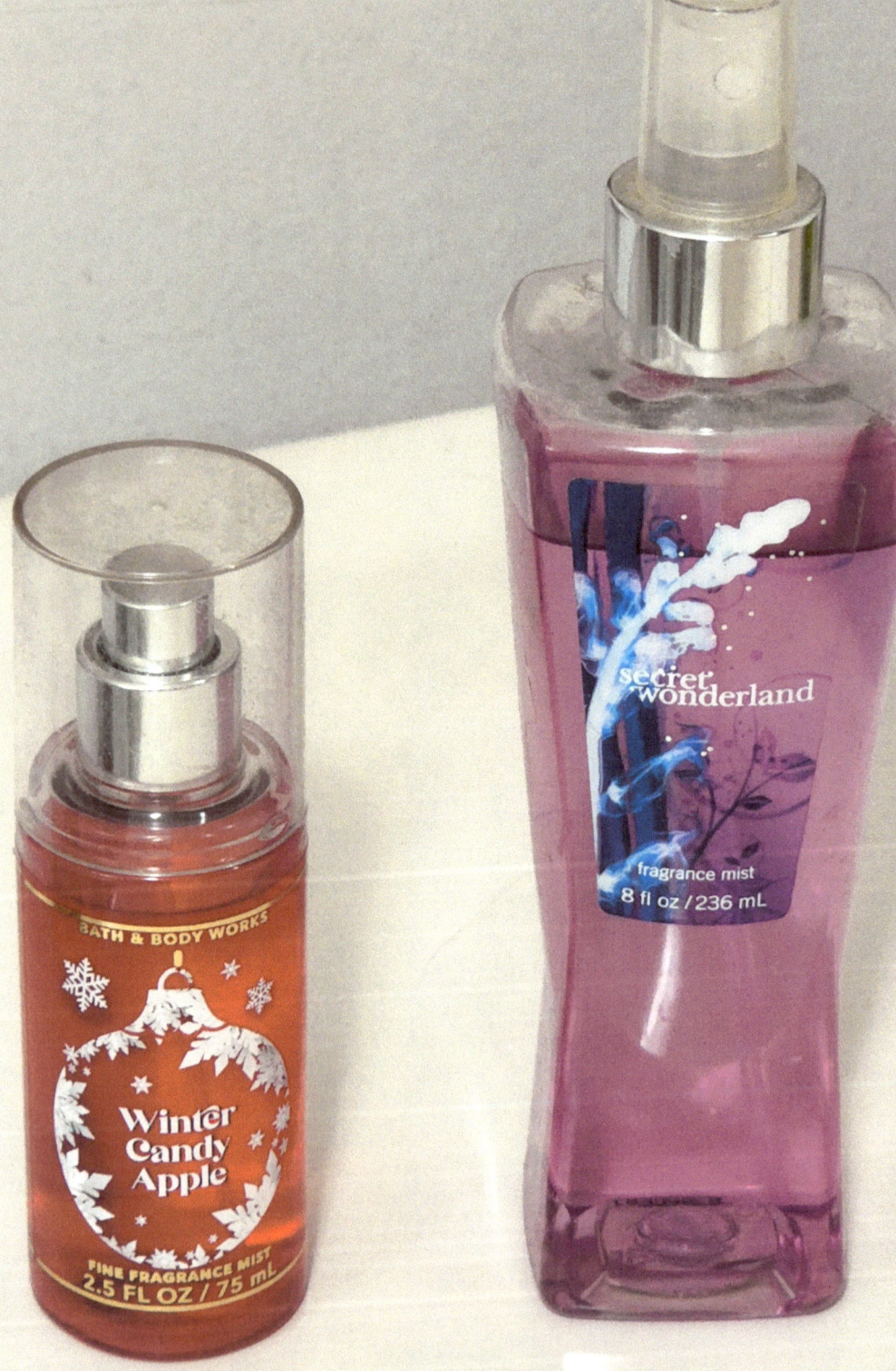

BATH & BODY WORKS

Winter
Candy
Apple

FINE FRAGRANCE MIST
2.5 FL OZ / 75 mL

secret
wonderland

fragrance mist
8 fl oz / 236 mL

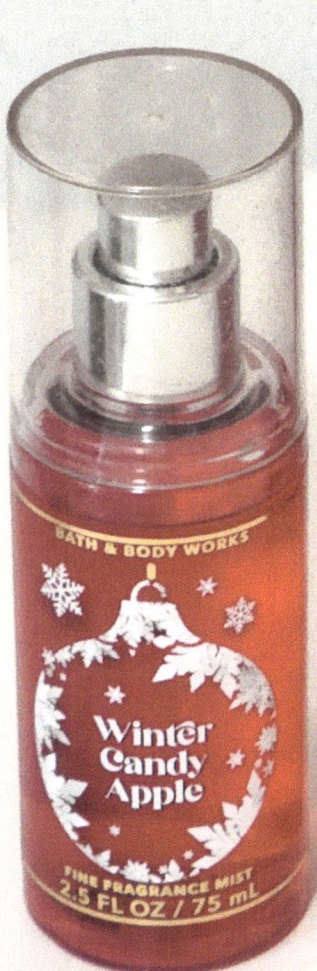
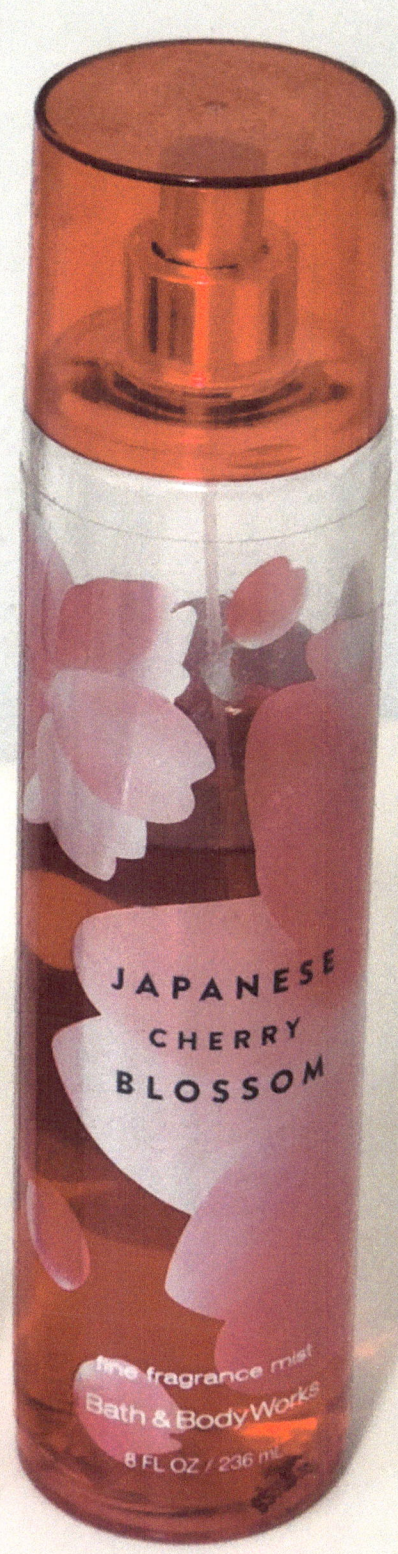

BATH & BODY WORKS

Winter Candy Apple

FINE FRAGRANCE MIST

2.5 FL OZ / 75 mL

JAPANESE CHERRY BLOSSOM

fine fragrance mist

Bath & BodyWorks

8 FL OZ / 236 mL

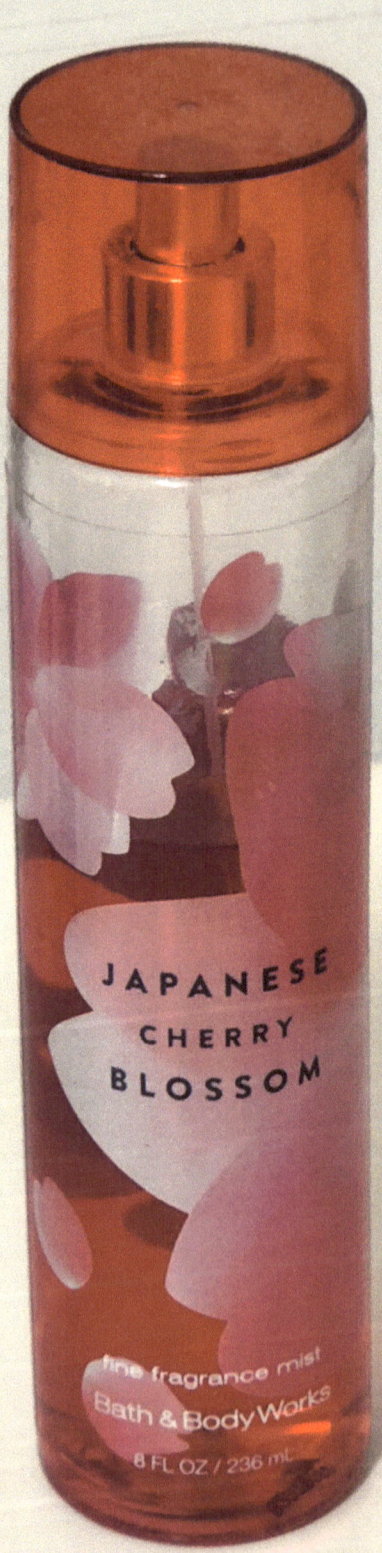

JAPANESE
CHERRY
BLOSSOM

fine fragrance mist

Bath & Body Works

8 FL OZ / 236 mL

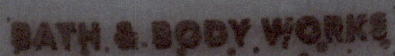
BATH & BODY WORKS

# Winter Candy Apple

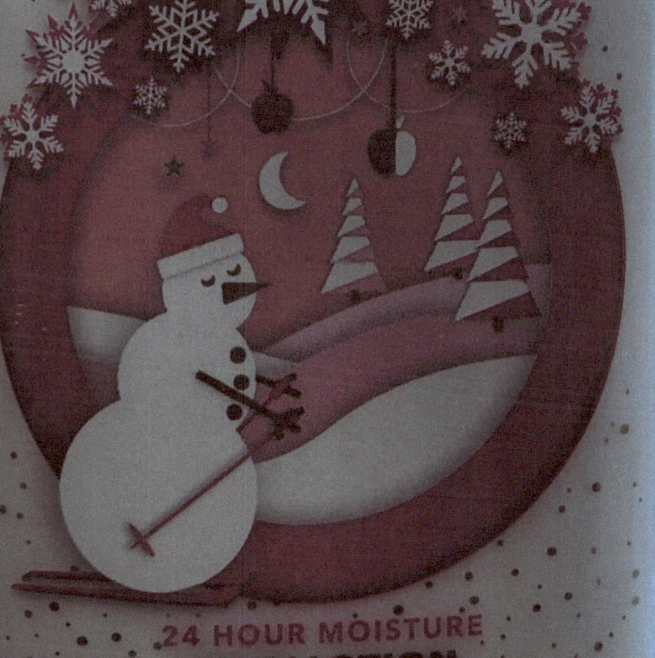

24 HOUR MOISTURE
## BODY LOTION
SHEA BUTTER + VITAMIN E
8 FL OZ / 236 mL

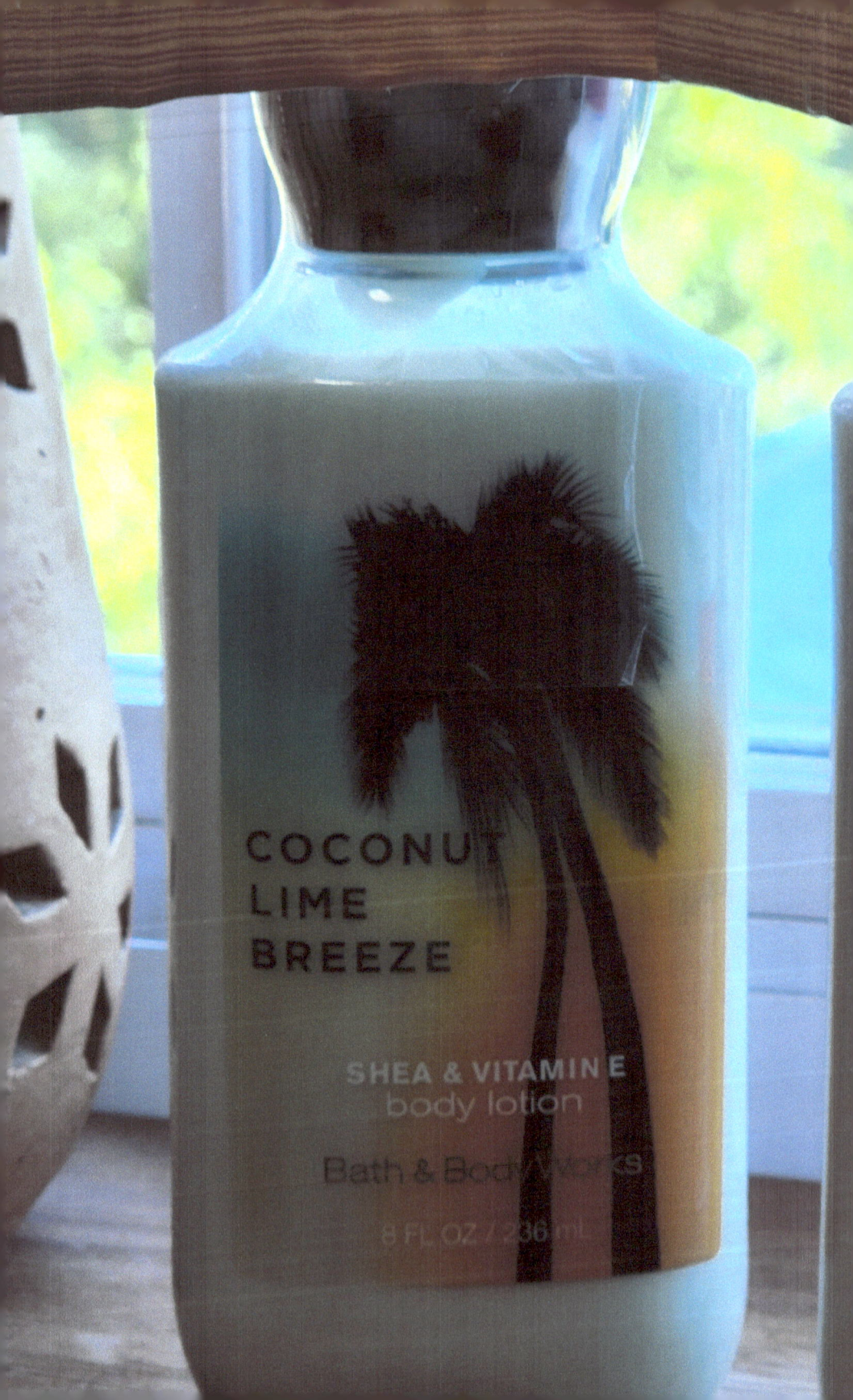

COCONUT
LIME
BREEZE

SHEA & VITAMIN E
body lotion

Bath & Body Works

8 FL OZ / 236 mL

# Winter Candy Apple

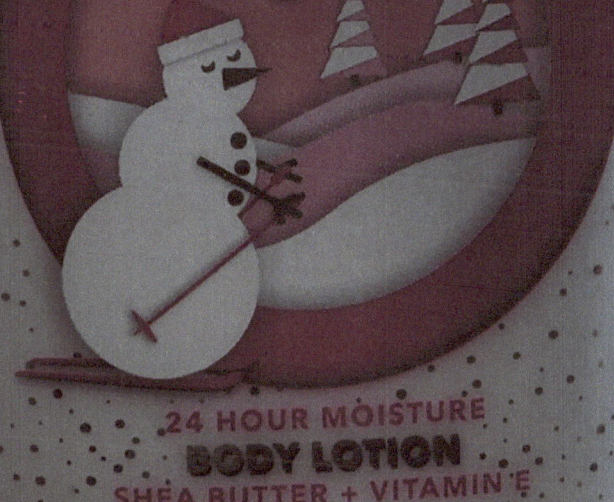

24 HOUR MOISTURE
## BODY LOTION
SHEA BUTTER + VITAMIN E
8 FL OZ / 236 mL

COCONUT
LIME
BREEZE

SHEA & VITAMIN E
body lotion

Bath & Body Works

8 FL OZ / 236 mL

BATH & BODY WORKS
Winter
Candy Apple

24 HOUR MOISTURE
BODY LOTION
SHEA BUTTER + VITAMIN E
8 FL OZ / 236 mL

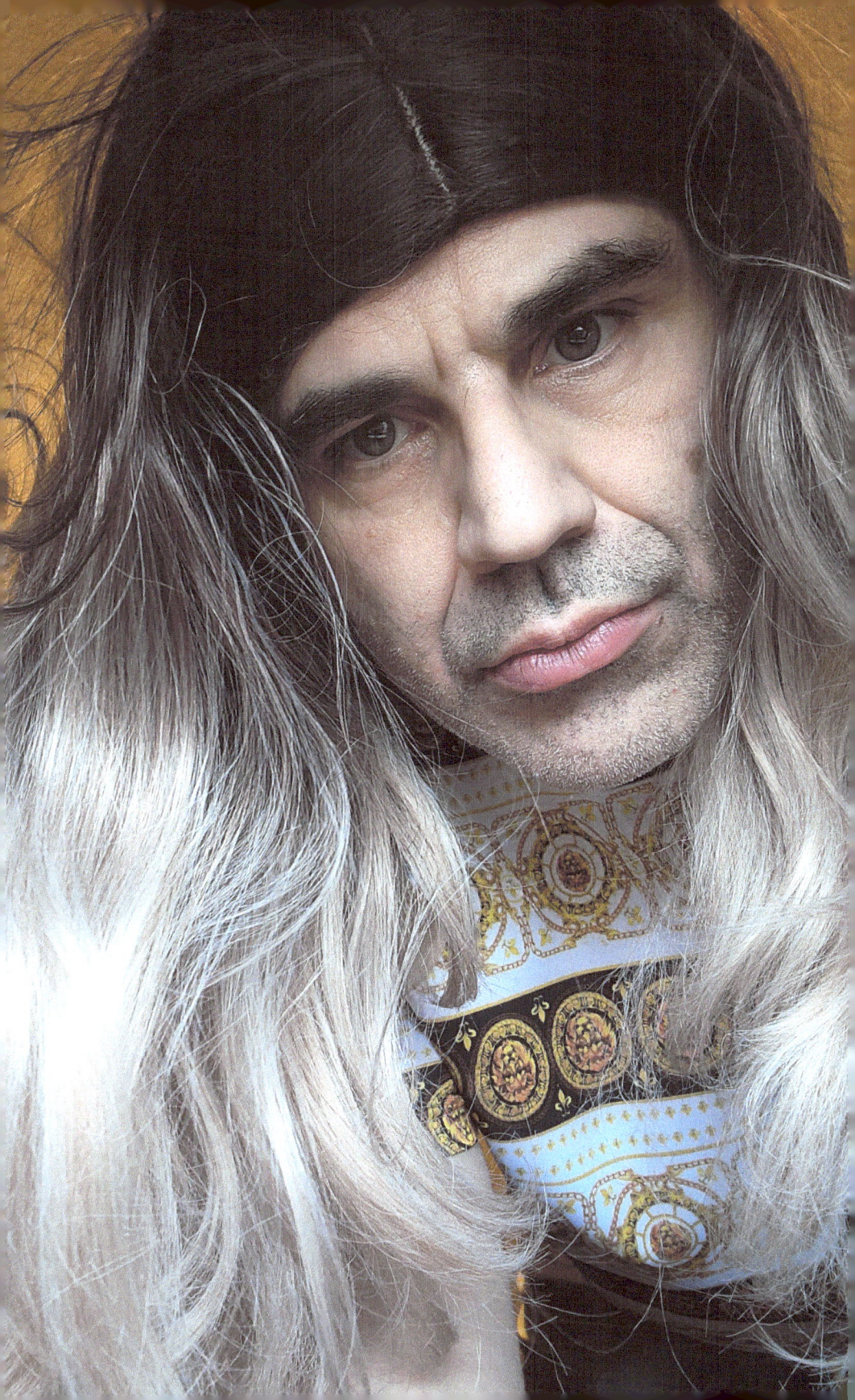

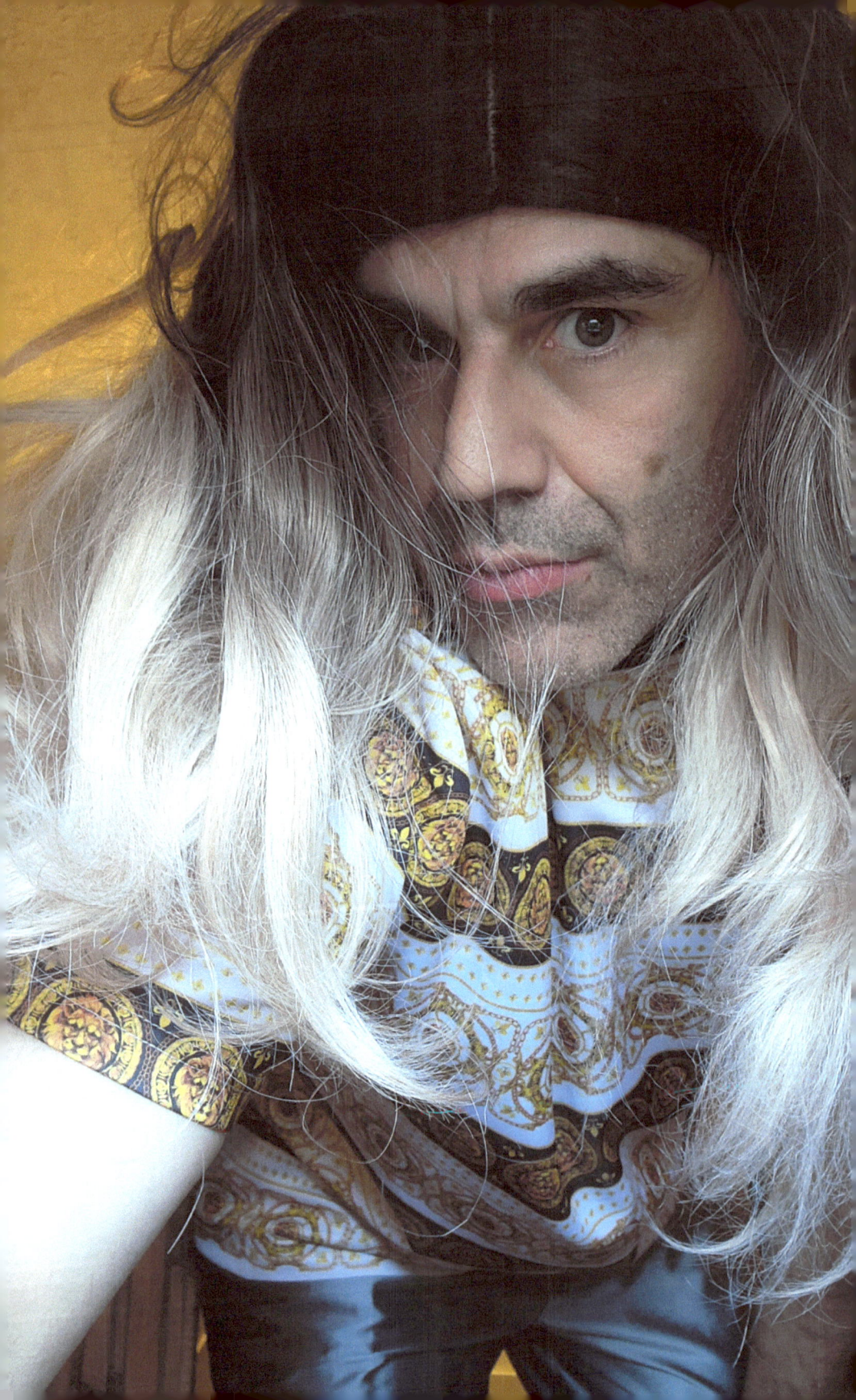

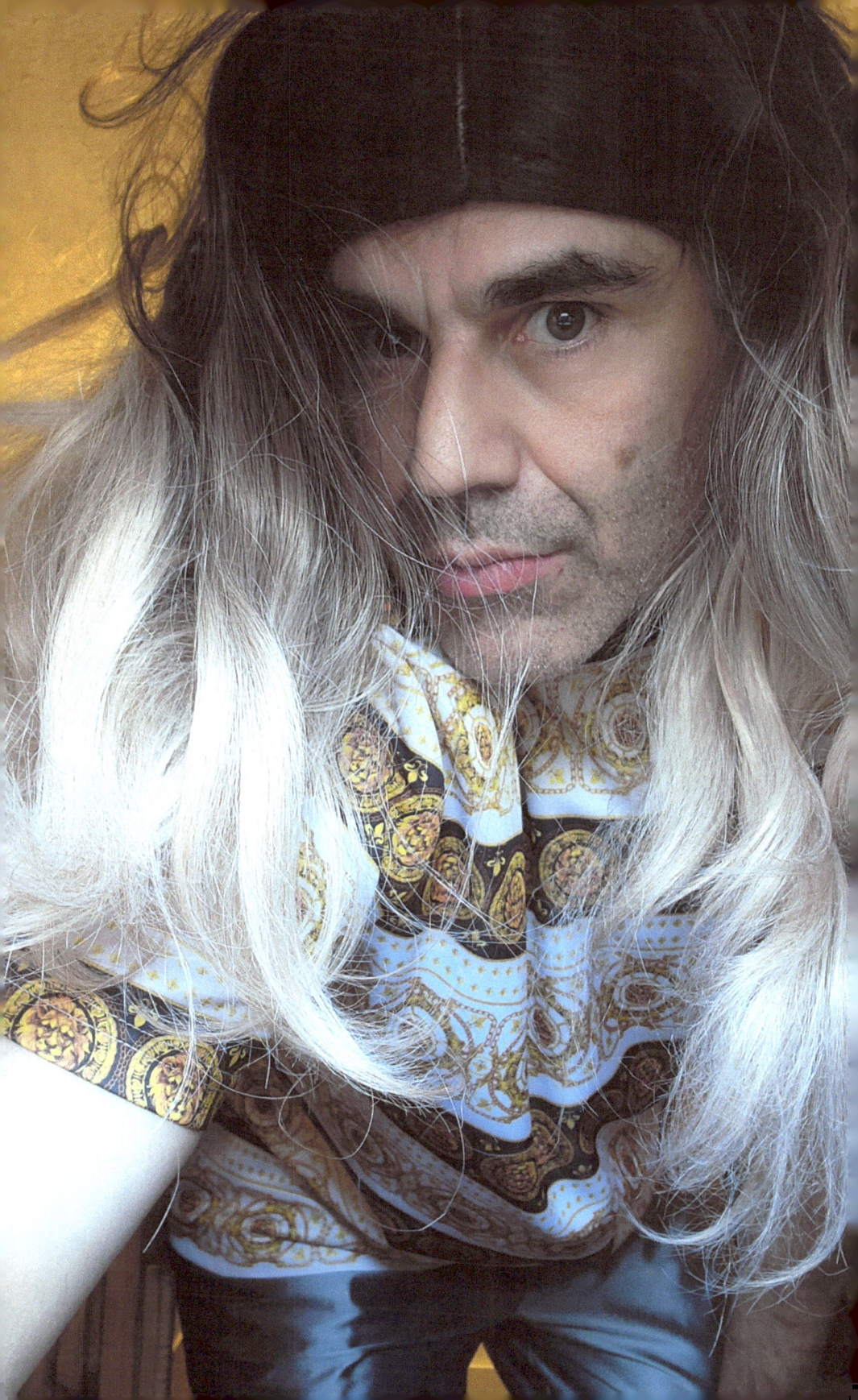

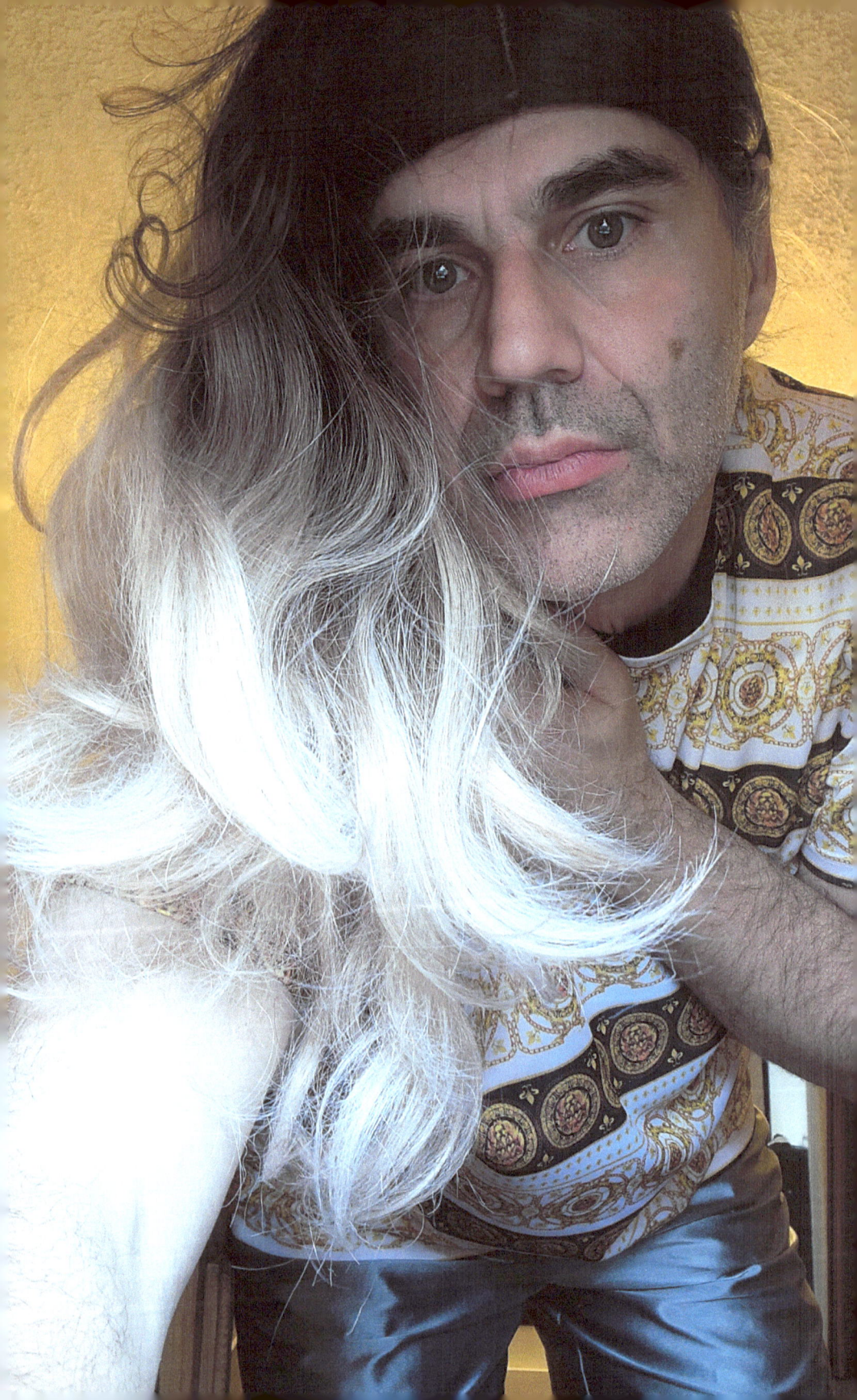

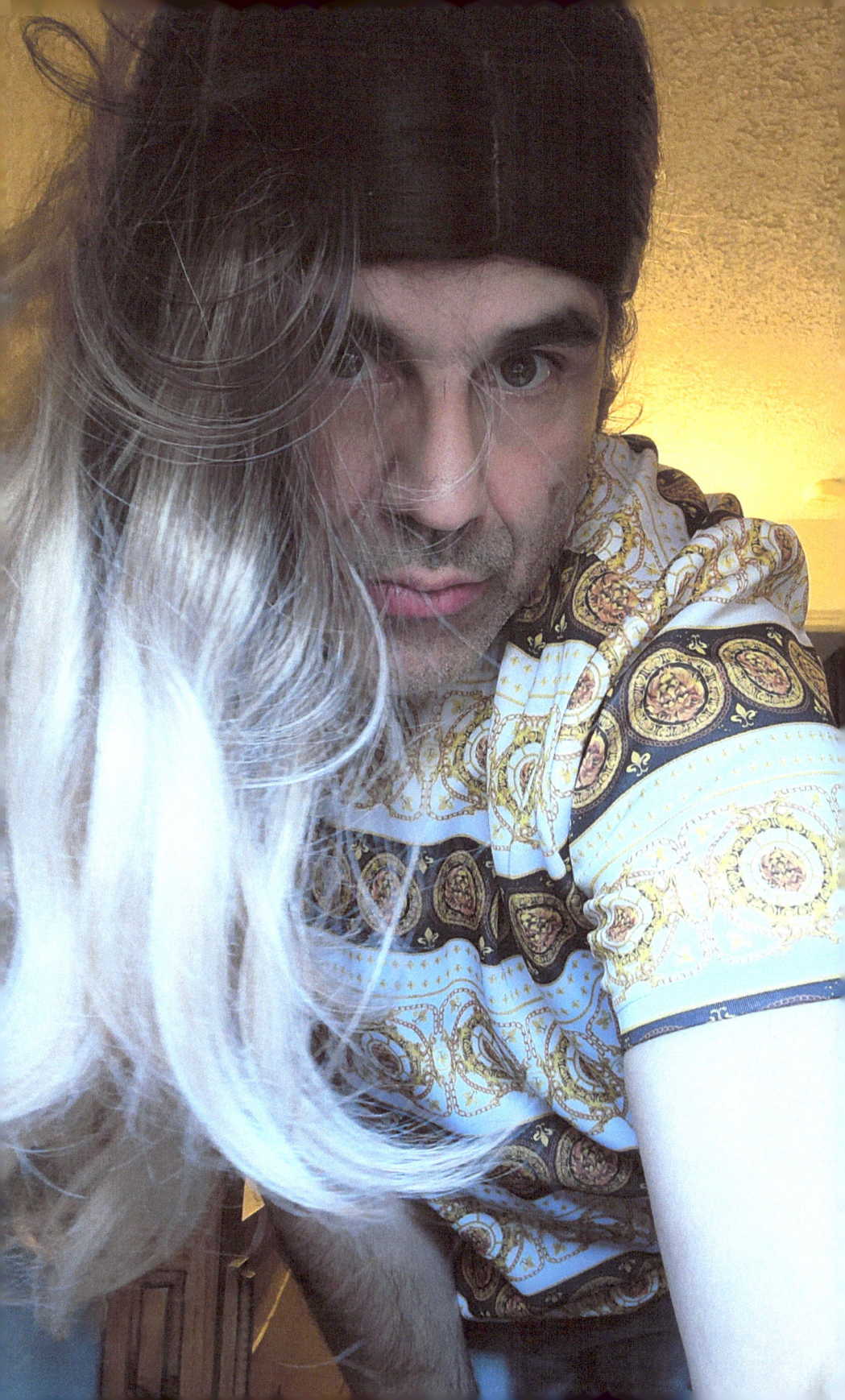

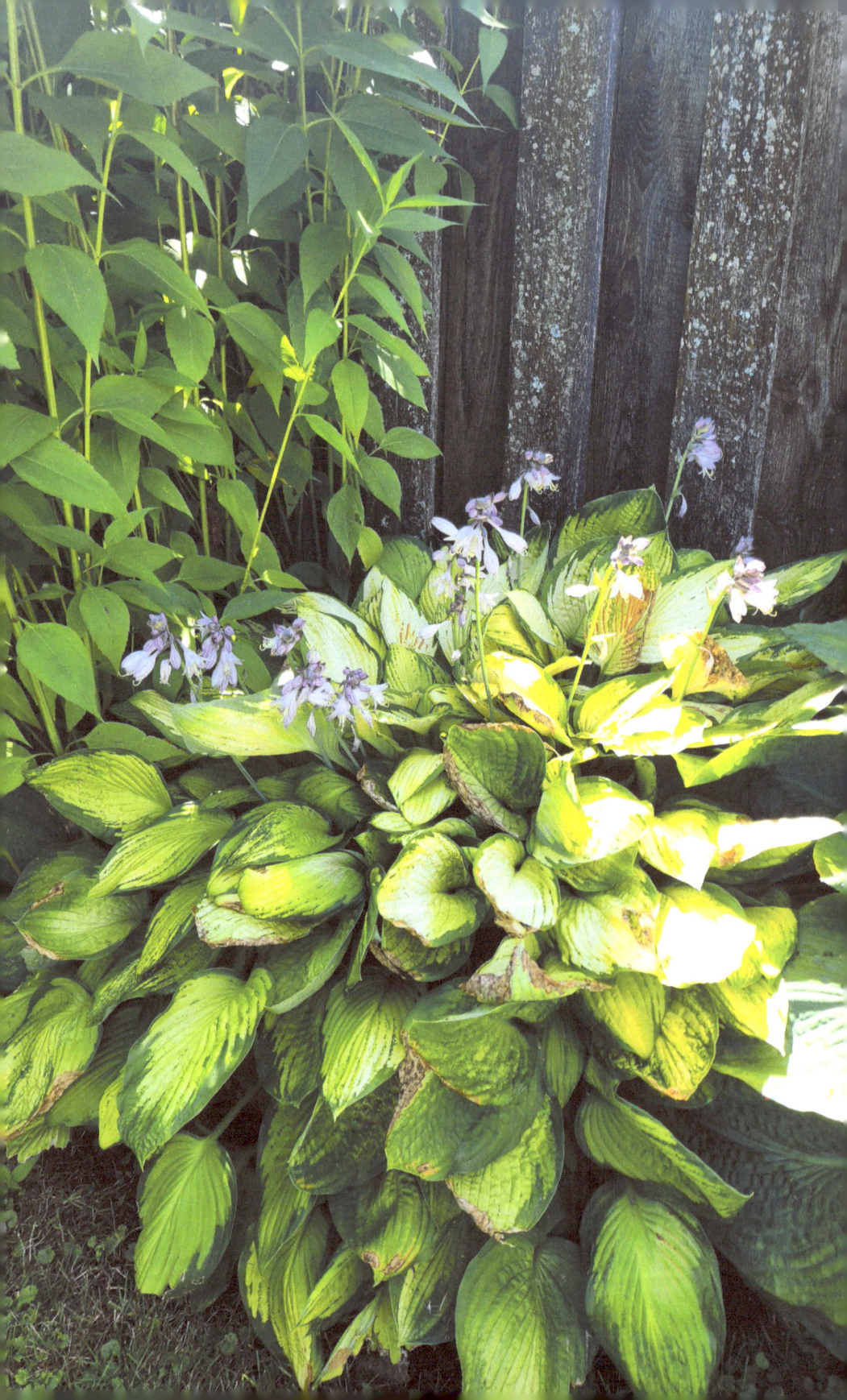

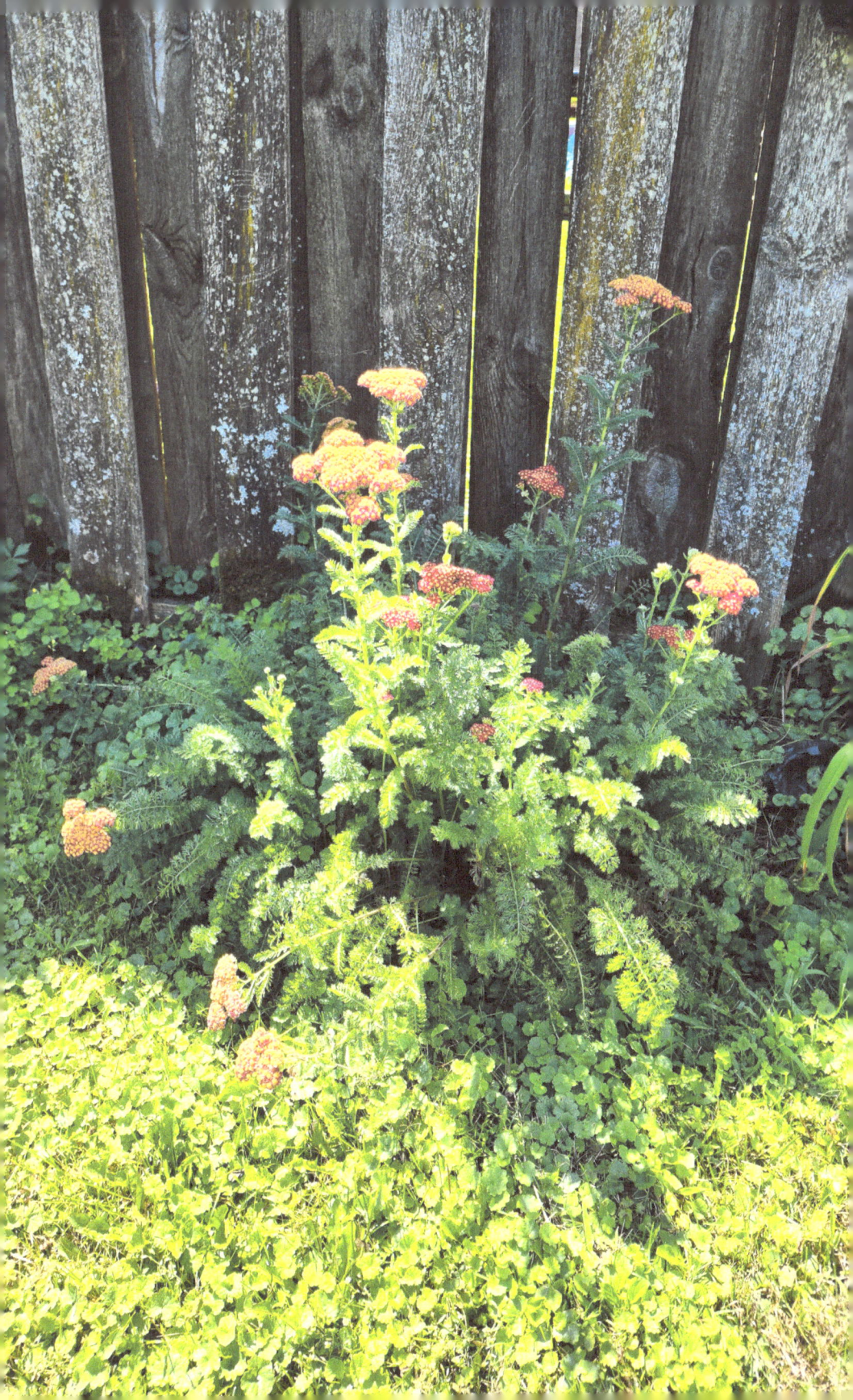

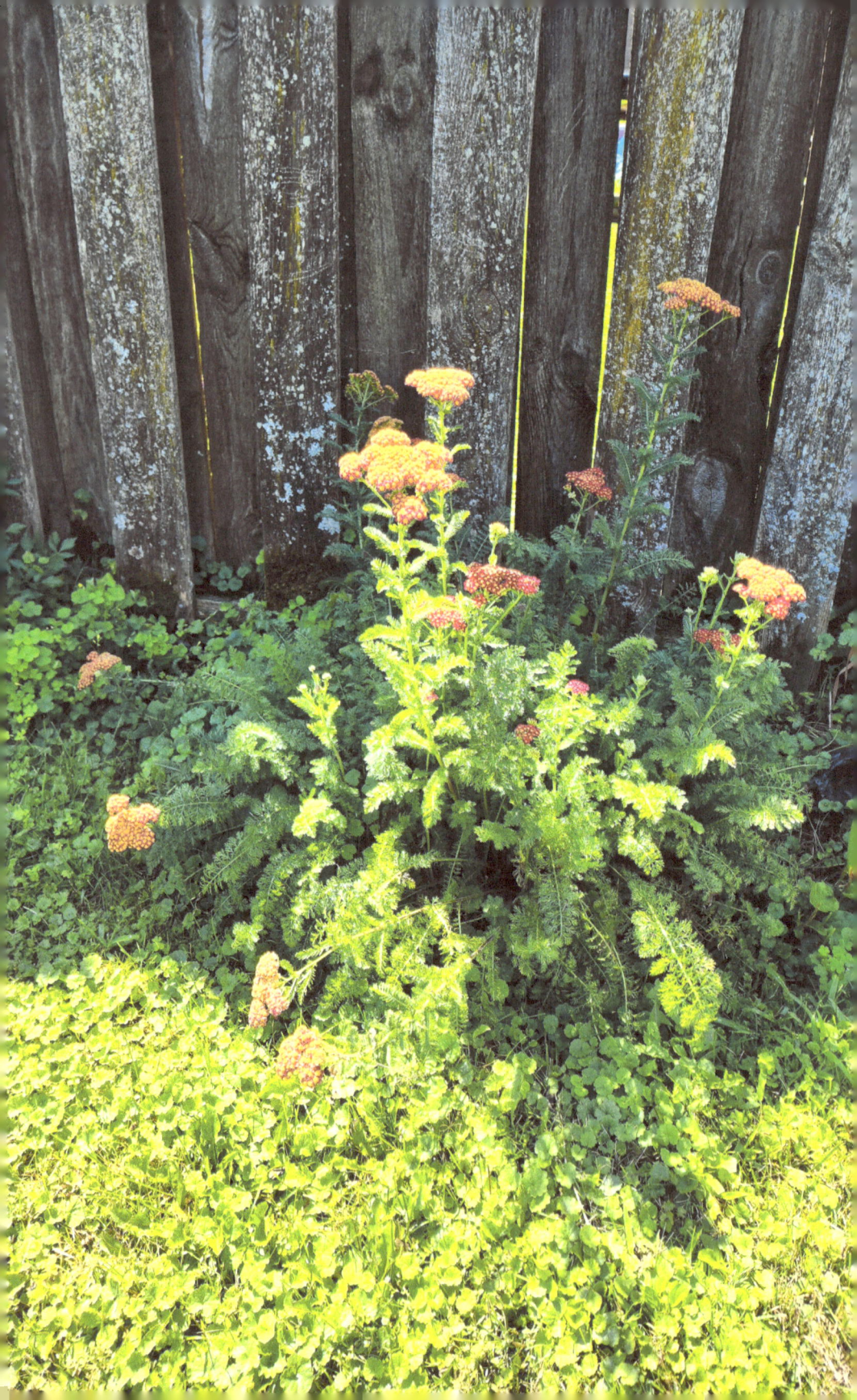

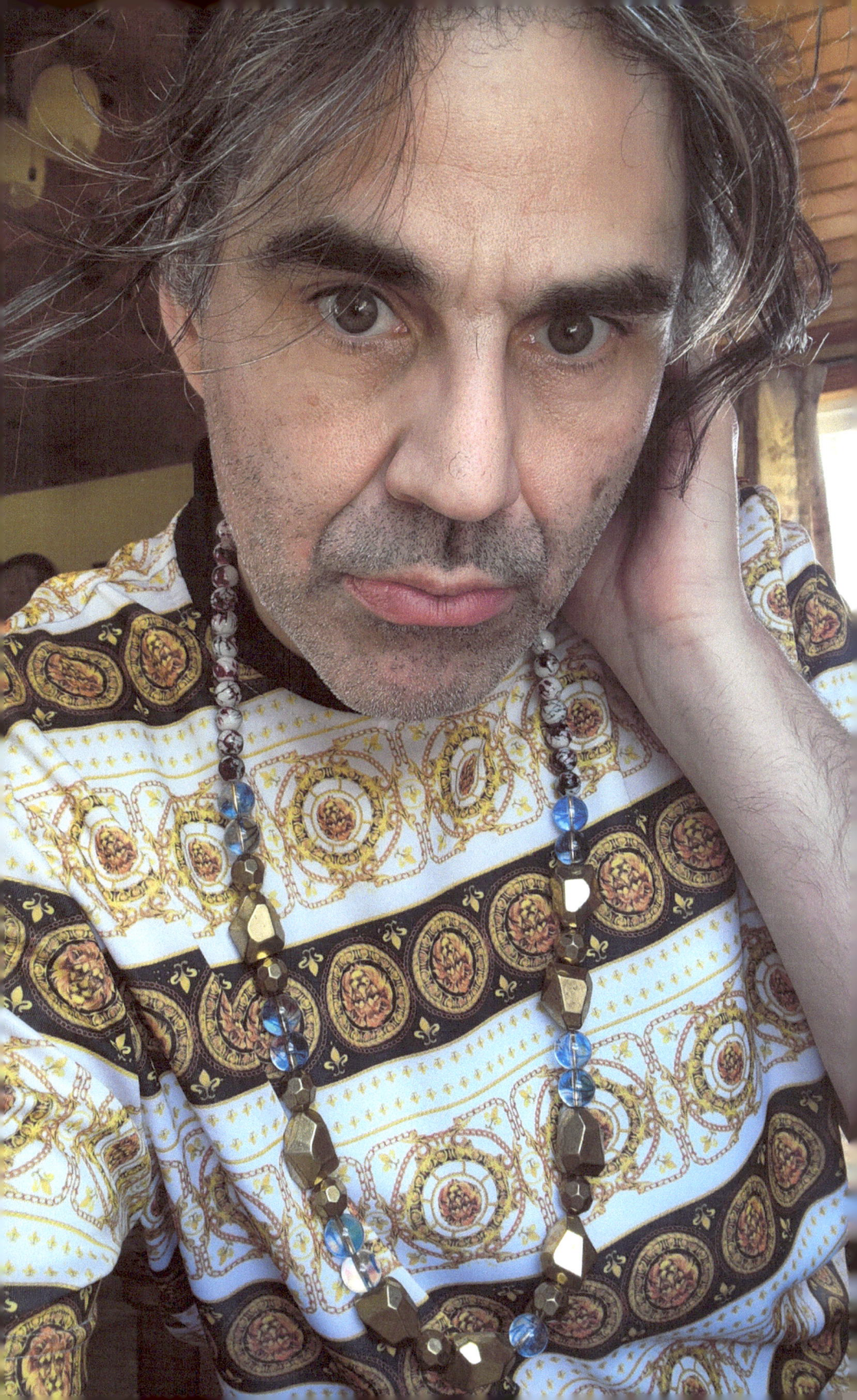

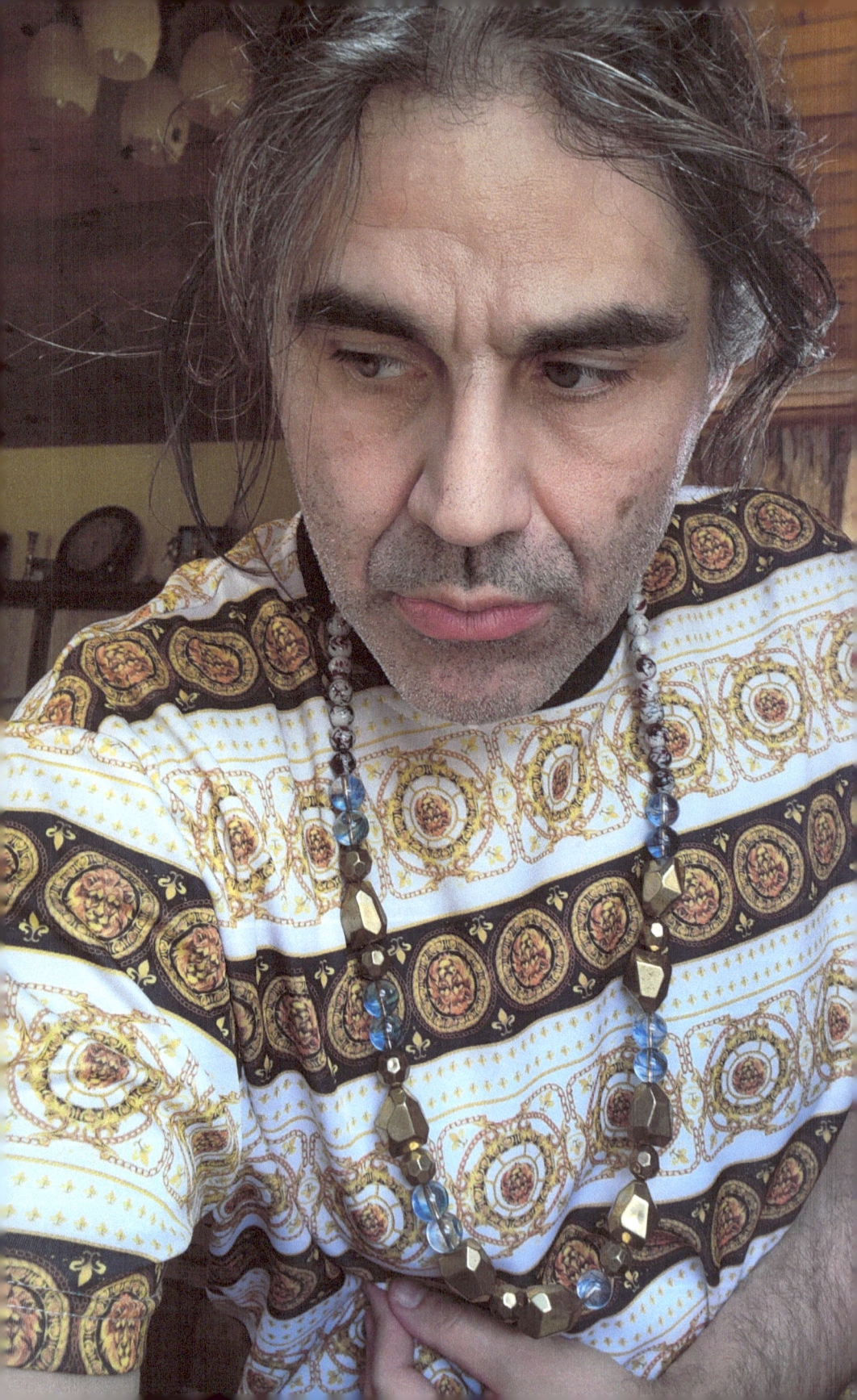

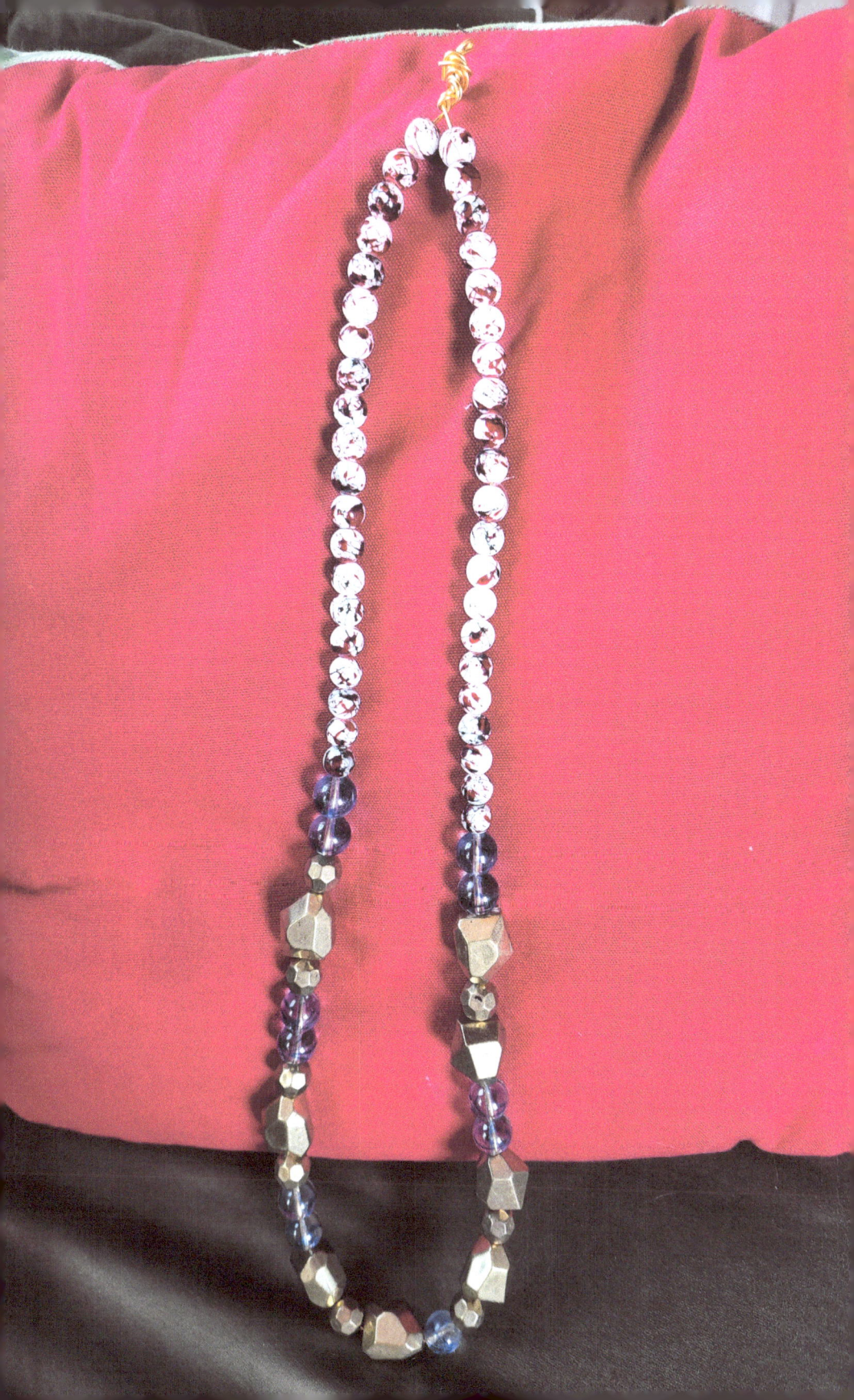

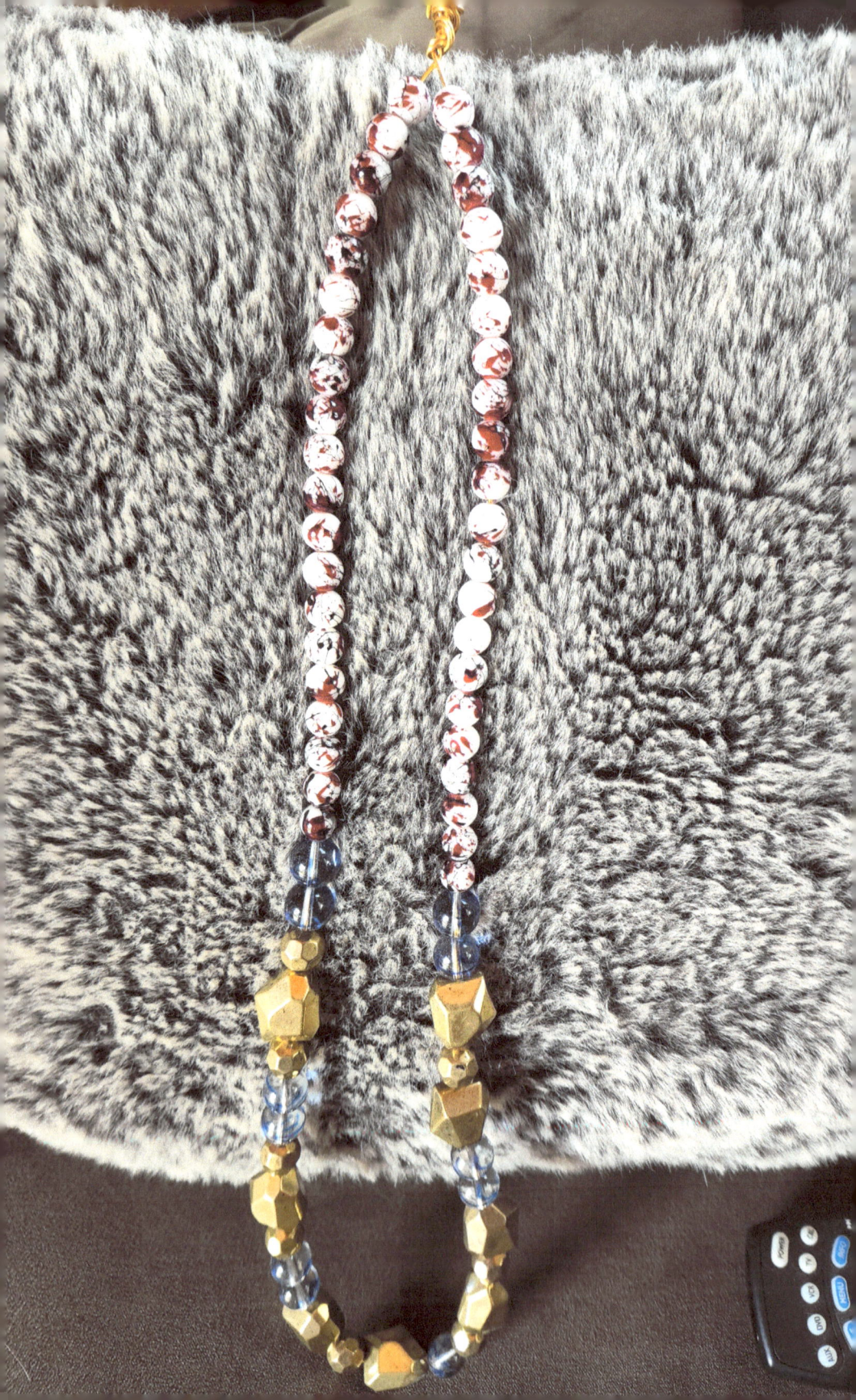

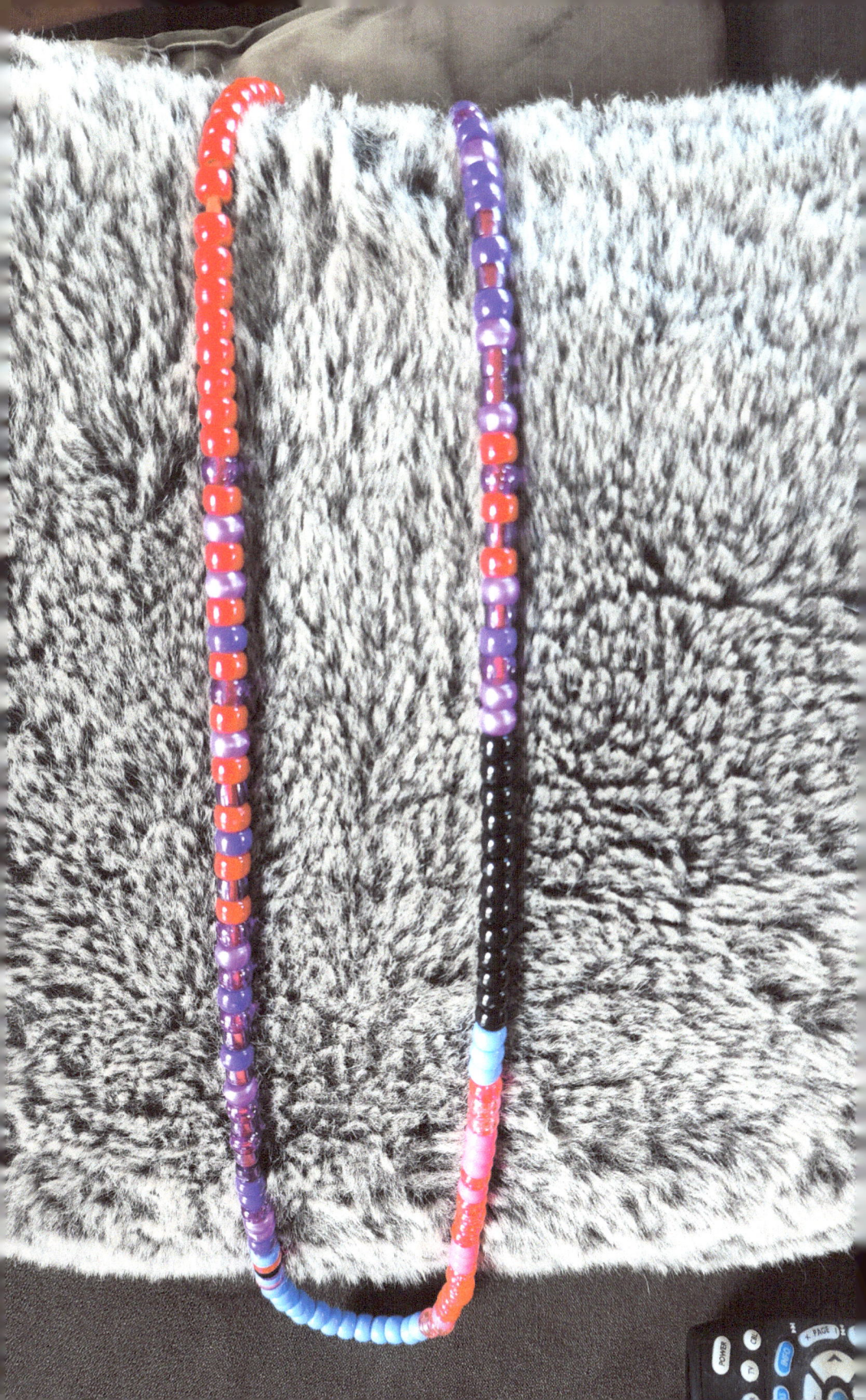

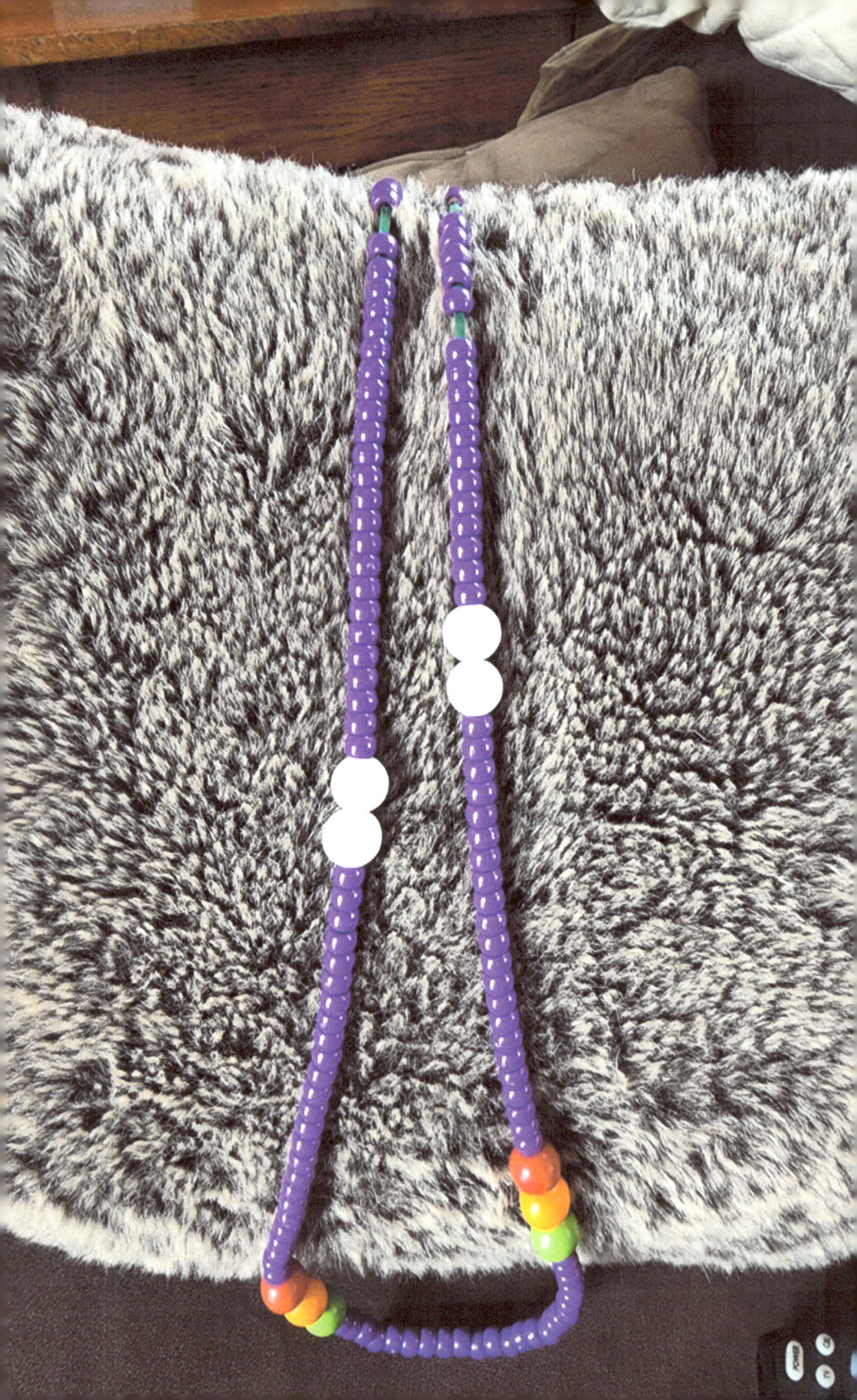

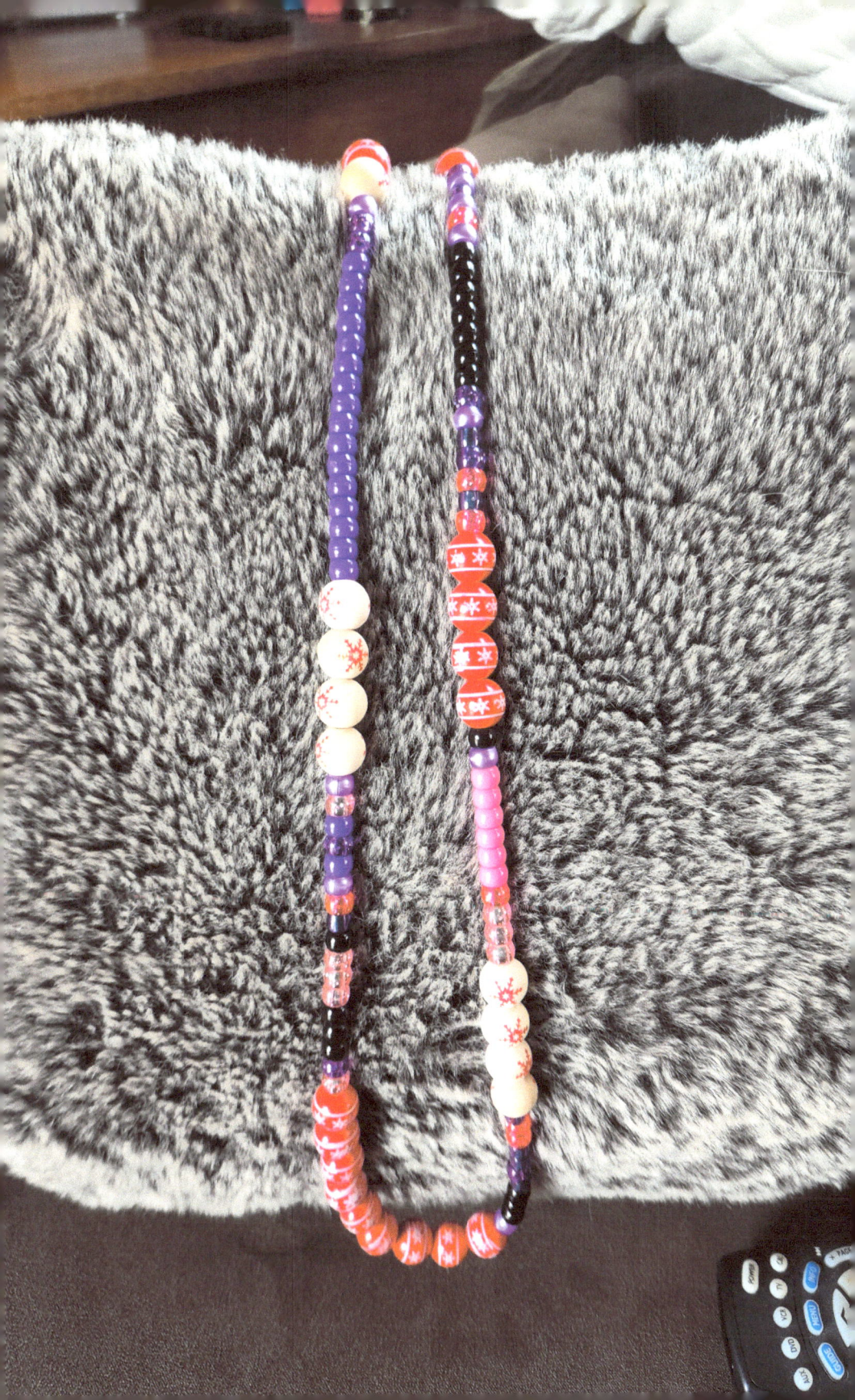